To Julia Child,

who proved to us that home cooking was

worthy of mastery and could rise to the

level of an art form.

chefs at HOME

Favorite Recipes from the Chefs
of Relais & Châteaux in North America

RELAIS &
CHATEAUX

NETWORK
BOOK PUBLISHING LTD

First published in 2010 by
Network Book Publishing Ltd.

Network House, 28 Ballmoor, Celtic Court,
Buckingham MK18 1RQ, UK

www.networkpublishingltd.com

© Network Book Publishing Ltd.

Printed by CT Printing Limited

ISBN No: 978-0-9562661-4-9

Printed in China

Publisher: Peter Marshall
Managing Editor and Art Director: Shirley Marshall
Editors: Sue Christelow, Katy Morris
Design Director: Philip Donnelly
Designer: Jemma Pentney
Photographer: Myburgh du Plessis

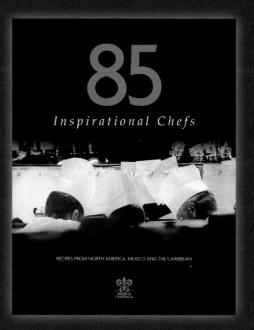

Most chefs crave simple, straightforward food when they eat at home.

These 69 North American chefs from the elite family of Relais & Châteaux are no exception. From nourishing soups to hearty burgers, these are some of their favorite, easy-to-make dishes when they're off duty. These recipes emphasize seasonality and sense of place. They reflect the fascinating geographic diversity in cooking styles across our vast continent and open a window into the minds of a fraternity of passionate masters of hospitality.

May they inspire you to entertain your family and friends with greater ease, imagination and confidence. It's reassuring to be reminded that oftentimes simpler can be better.

We look forward to welcoming you to the world of Relais & Châteaux.

Patrick O'Connell

President of North American Relais & Châteaux Delegations
Chef/Proprietor of The Inn at Little Washington

Welcome

to Chefs at Home, the cookbook with a difference.

AT RELAIS & CHATEAUX we pride ourselves on our family values. A family of hoteliers and Grands Chefs around the world, we have a commitment to ensuring that our guests feel as comfortable and relaxed as they would be in their own home. This family mentality has meant that each member of the Relais & Châteaux group offers special moments and unforgettable experiences while maintaining this unique philosophy.

Chefs at Home is a compilation of recipes from Chefs and Grands Chefs from Relais & Châteaux properties in North America, Mexico and the Caribbean. Known for producing exemplary cuisine, the Chefs of Relais & Châteaux are regularly complimented on the quality of their food. Offering exquisitely fresh ingredients of the highest caliber with equal technical skill there is no doubt that these Chefs have it all in the way of culinary expertise.

However, even Chefs need to go home, spend time with their own families and enjoy the comfort that home brings. The recipes in *Chefs at Home* have been selected to honor the 'at-home' Chef, the dishes these culinary masters choose to cook when they are at home. In an original take on the traditional cookbook, the Chefs and Grands Chefs of Relais & Châteaux have chosen to share with you their most cherished at-home dishes, family dinners and baking favorites.

Follow your favorite Chefs as they explain their choice of home dish and impress your own family as you recreate these superb recipes at home. Whether you are looking for a quick hunger fix or a dinner party staple the extensive range of recipes in *Chefs at Home* ensures that there is something for everyone.

Separated into four major sections consisting of 'Starters, and Soups', 'Fish, Seafood and Crustacean Main Dishes', 'Meat, Game and Poultry Main Dishes' and 'Desserts' there is a wide range of choice available. Plus there is also an additional section of at-home favorites that are perfect any time of day! The 'And Finally...' section of the book shows a range of simple baking treats that can be shared with all the family.

Every recipe features a note on why the Chef has chosen his home dish.

Whether it is originally inspired from a family member's traditional recipe, to encourage people to try new ingredients or a popular hotel dish that everyone asks for, read the story behind these culinary choices. As well as this each Chef has submitted a short biography about his life and hobbies, so you can really get to know him out of the kitchen.

These iconic Relais & Châteaux Chefs have ensured that each recipe is clear and simple to follow. Scattered throughout the book, selected Chefs have provided a Chef's tip, to really help with your cooking. From tried and tested methods to possible ingredient alternatives, the Chefs' tips really add to the recipe, making you feel as if the Chef is in the kitchen with you!

All recipes are fully illustrated to help guide you into creating a dish that looks as good as it tastes, while the brief introduction tells you a little bit more about the background of the dish, so you can impress your dinner guests with your knowledge, or simply to satisfy your own curiosity.

With *Chefs at Home* you can be part of the Relais & Châteaux family, and give your family and friends the real Relais & Châteaux experience in your own home while taking a part in the food that these inspirational Chefs really love.

RELAIS &
CHATEAUX.

CONTENTS

STARTERS & SOUPS

Start as you mean to go on with this great selection of starters and soups. Whether offering the perfect introduction to a dinner party or just a bite to eat after a long day, this section has all you need in soups and starters.

Customer favorites and at-home staples have been chosen to really kick-start your evening. Choose from a wide selection including Grand Chef Jason Robinson's comforting 'Ricotta Gnocchi' or Grand Chef Normand Laprise's unique take on a 'BLT'; here there is something for vegetarians and meat eaters alike. Enjoy finding out the secrets of starters with these great chefs.

BUTTERNUT SQUASH BISQUE

BY GARY DANKO

Butternut squash, apples and a touch of honey. This soup can be enjoyed plain and simple or lends well to many types of garnishes. The photo shown is garnished with Dungeness crab and a chive biscuit. You could also use chicken, smoked duck or some cheese. If you are not fond of butternut squash, try pumpkin.

GARY DANKO

I live in San Francisco in the Russian Hill neighborhood with my partner, although I am originally from a small town in upstate New York called Massena.

Butternut squash bisque is one of the restaurant's signature Fall dishes – the soup is very delicious, very healthy and easy to make. It can be served in a very simple way or enhanced with different garnishes as it blends well with many different flavors.

My favorite ingredients are branzini or Mediterranean Sea bass, as well as duck, quail, avocados, mangos, passion fruit, oysters, mussels and clams and also the most versatile of foods – eggs.

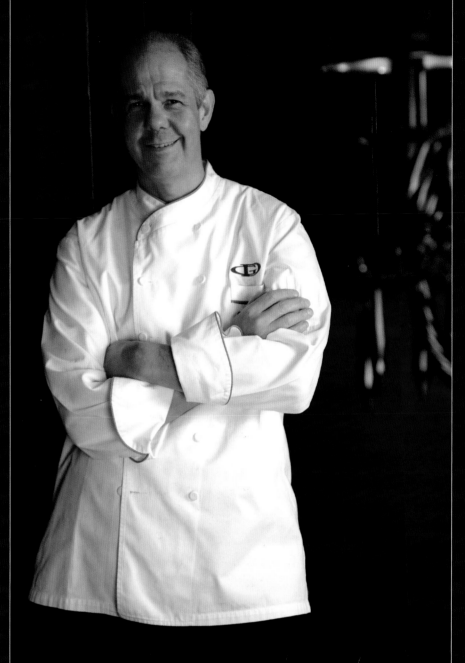

"very delicious, very healthy and easy to make"

BUTTERNUT SQUASH BISQUE

BY GARY DANKO

serves 6-8

ingredients

4 tbsp	butter
1	large onion (4 oz), peeled and diced
2 lb	butternut squash, peeled, seeded and cut into 1" cubes
2	golden delicious apples, peeled and cored
2 qt	chicken stock or water
1	bay leaf
1	sprig of thyme
2 tbsp	honey
½ tsp	kosher salt (or to taste)

to serve:

½ tsp	ground pepper
½ cup	Cheddar, Asiago or fontina cheese, grated (optional)

method

Melt the butter in a large pot. Add the onion and sauté until translucent; this sweetens the onion. Add the squash and the apples and sauté for a few more minutes. Cover with the stock and add the bay leaf, thyme, and honey. Salt lightly, bring to a boil, and simmer until the squash is very soft, about 25 minutes.

Remove the bay leaf and thyme. Purée the soup in a food processor or run it through the food mill. The blender will have a more velvety texture, the food mill more coarse.

to serve:

Return the soup to the pot. Add the pepper and, if desired, the cheese. Stir over a low flame until the cheese is melted and the soup is piping hot. Serve.

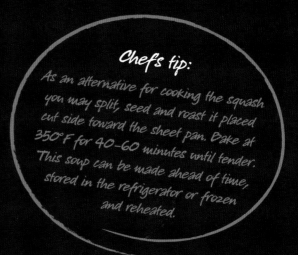

Chef's tip:

As an alternative for cooking the squash you may split, seed and roast it placed cut side toward the sheet pan. Bake at 350°F for 40–60 minutes until tender. This soup can be made ahead of time, stored in the refrigerator or frozen and reheated.

15

BARRON POINT OYSTER GRATIN,
CREAMED SPINACH, PARMESAN MOUSSE, PANCETTA CRISP
BY KARSTEN HART

This is one of my favorite dishes to cook at home. It's fast, simple and delicious. In one bite you have the salty brine from the oyster, richness from the cheese and mushrooms, a little acid and heat from the Tabasco. Delicious!

KARSTEN HART

I just recently married my beautiful wife Deja with whom I reside at the gateway of the most breathtaking area of California, Yosemite National Park. I enjoy many hobbies such as photography, mountain biking, running, and hiking and on occasion fly-fishing in the Sierra Nevada mountain range.

I have chosen the baked oyster dish because it reminds me of my childhood years growing up in Louisiana where oysters are a staple product in many dishes. My Louisiana upbringing was influential on my decision to become a professional chef as cooking is a large part of Louisiana culture – everyone proudly boasts their own gumbo recipe! Now, when I get homesick, I cook something Cajun and it takes me back to the bayou.

My favorite ingredient is salt. It has many functions including aiding the release of water for sweating, curing products and pickling. Salt is used to control the fermentation rate of yeast, aids in the strengthening of gluten in bread dough, indeed salt enhances flavor in everything; it's the king of all ingredients!

Chef's tip:
Inspect the oysters for health and weight. Fresh live oysters should always feel heavy for their size (due to their full state of hydration) and should either be tightly closed or close quickly when provoked. If cleaning oysters for later use, store on ice in a well drained pan.

BARRON POINT OYSTER GRATIN,
CREAMED SPINACH, PARMESAN MOUSSE, PANCETTA CRISP

BY KARSTEN HART

serves 4

ingredients

oysters:

12	fresh oysters, alive and in their shell

creamed spinach:

1 tbsp	bacon, ground
1 tbsp	butter
1 cup	king oyster mushrooms, sliced
1	shallot, minced
1	clove garlic, minced
2	ribs celery, with leaves removed and minced
1	green bell pepper, cored, seeded and finely diced
1 qt	spinach leaves, washed
	oyster liquor
¼ cup	dry white wine
½ cup	heavy cream
1 tbsp	chopped parsley
	Tabasco sauce
	Worcestershire sauce
	salt & freshly ground black pepper

parmesan mousse:

1 tbsp	butter
1	shallot, minced
1	parsnip, peeled and small diced
2 cups	heavy cream
1	large parmesan rind
¼ cup	prosciutto scraps
3	sprigs of thyme

gratin for the oysters:

½ cup	panko breadcrumbs, ground
¼ cup	parmesan cheese, grated
	salt & freshly ground black pepper

pancetta crisps:

12	thin pancetta slices

to serve:

lemon juice
Tabasco sauce

method

oysters:

Clean and shuck the oysters. Reserve the liquor. Leave the oyster in the bottom of the shell, ensuring that it has been separated.

creamed spinach:

Over a low heat in a medium heavy bottomed pot, render the bacon and butter completely. Turn up the heat and add the mushrooms. Cook until just starting to lightly brown. Add the shallot, garlic, celery and pepper. Sauté for another minute or until soft. Season. Add the spinach, oyster liquor, wine, cream, and parsley, and reduce by half. Season with the Tabasco, Worcestershire sauce, salt and pepper. Remove from the heat and reserve.

parmesan mousse:

In a small sauce pot over a medium heat, sauté the shallot in butter until translucent. Add the parsnip and continue to cook until soft. Add the cream, parmesan, prosciutto, and thyme and simmer for 30 minutes. Remove from the heat and purée in a food processor. Pass through a fine chinois. Pour the mixture into a thermo whip and charge. Reserve for later.

gratin for the oysters:

In a stainless steel bowl mix all the ingredients thoroughly. Reserve for later.

pancetta crisps:

Preheat the oven to 400°F. Place the pancetta slices on a silpat and bake in the oven for 5 minutes or until crispy. Reserve for later.

to serve:

Preheat the oven to 425°F. Spoon creamed spinach over each oyster. Top with the gratin mixture and bake until golden brown. Season each oyster with lemon juice and Tabasco. Place three oysters on each of four preheated plates. Using a thermo whip, form parmesan mousse clouds on top of each oyster. Finish with a pancetta crisp.

RISOTTO OF WOODLAND MUSHROOMS
AND ROASTED CELERY ROOT

BY LEE PARSONS

The perfect comfort food, simple yet elegant and versatile depending on the season. Enjoy the risotto with fresh morels in the Spring, delicate chanterelles in the Summer or tasty porcini in the Fall.

LEE PARSONS

I was born and raised in the historic town of Wilton, South of England and I currently reside on the west side of Vancouver. When I am not in the kitchen, I can often be found fishing, mountain biking or shopping for baby clothes with my wife for our twin girls.

I have chosen a risotto recipe because of its elegant simplicity. The dish is versatile and can be changed according to flavor preferences. My personal preference and favorite ingredient is wild mushrooms. Depending on the season, I typically enjoy my risotto with fresh morels in the Spring, delicate chanterelles in the Summer, or tasty porcini in the Fall. Another reason why I chose risotto is because it only requires one pan! As the official chef and dishwasher in my own home, I know the importance of kitchen efficiency.

Chef's tip:

Any seasonal woodland or cultivated mushroom works well for the risotto. It can also be enhanced with a few drops of truffle oil.

10½ oz	celery root (celeriac), small dice
3½ oz	butter
	salt & pepper
2 pt	white chicken stock
1	shallot, finely chopped
5¼ oz	mixed woodland mushrooms, including golden chanterelles, yellow foot, shamiji
1 tsp	olive oil
3½ oz	onions, finely chopped
1	garlic clove, finely chopped
1	sprig of fresh thyme
10½ oz	carnaroli risotto rice
3½ fl oz	white wine
2 oz	grana padano cheese, grated
2 tbsp	mixed chopped herbs, including chervil, parsley, chives and tarragon
	squeeze of fresh lemon juice

to serve:

grana padano cheese, freshly shaved
sautéed mushrooms
chervil sprigs

Preheat the oven to 350ºF. Sweat the celery root in 1 oz of the butter. Season with salt and pepper. Place into the oven and cook until soft, approximately 30 minutes. Using a hand blender, purée the celery root until smooth, then reserve.

Bring the white chicken stock to a simmer in a separate pan. Sauté the chopped shallot and mushrooms in the olive oil. Season to taste. Remove from the pan and put to one side until finishing the risotto.

Sweat the onions and garlic in the remaining 2½ oz butter with the thyme until soft. Add the rice, increase the heat and toast for 2-3 minutes. Add the white wine and half of the stock, continually stirring the risotto mix until the rice starts to absorb the liquid. Add the remaining liquid in small amounts – it will take approximately 18-20 minutes to cook. Once the rice is cooked remove from the heat. Add the shallot/mushrooms, puréed celery root, cheese and chopped herbs. Season to taste with salt, pepper and a good squeeze of fresh lemon.

to serve:

Divide the risotto into even portions in the center of a plate or bowl. Finish with the cheese, mushrooms and chervil sprigs.

"I look at raw products to get inspiration and like to use traditional local ingredients"

TORTILLA SOUP

BY MAURICIO ESPINOSA

*This soup is a traditional
dish at Las Mañanitas.*

MAURICIO ESPINOSA

I was born in Tuxtla Gutierrez, Chiapas and I now live in Cuernavaca, Morelos. I studied at the Euroamerica Gastronomic School in Cuernavaca. My favorite ingredients are spices in general — they really make a dish! I especially like star anise, pepper, curcuma and curry.

I have chosen this dish as it is really popular in the restaurant and easy to make at home. I'm 100% dedicated to my main passion which is being a gastronomic architect, but my hobbies are sports, especially extreme climbing, as well as mountain cycling.

"**this dish is really popular in the restaurant and easy to make at home**"

TORTILLA SOUP

BY MAURICIO ESPINOSA

serves 1

ingredients

1 tbsp	corn oil
¼ cup	chopped onion
1	clove of garlic, finely chopped
2	guajillo chilies
1	ancho chili
1	large tomato
3 cups	chicken broth, extra if needed
4	sprigs of epazote
salt, to taste	

to serve:

2	tortillas, cut into strips
1	chili pasilla, cut in strips
1	Hass avocado, chopped
¼ cup	farmers cheese or fresh cheese
2 tbsp	cream
2 tbsp	crumbled pork crackling (fried pork skin)

method

In a frying pan gently heat the oil and fry the onion and garlic for 2-3 minutes, add the chilies, and fry for a further minute. Add the tomato and cook for a further 5-6 minutes, or until the tomato is cooked through. Add 1 cup of chicken broth and leave to simmer until the sauce thickens and becomes concentrated. Leave to cool, blend and sieve. Then add the rest of the chicken broth and the epazote to the sieved mixture. Simmer for about 10 minutes or until the broth has developed a good taste. Adjust the seasoning to taste.

to serve:

Fry the tortilla strips until golden in color, drain off any excess oil on paper towel. Fry the chili pasilla and drain on paper towel. Add all ingredients to the soup bowl as decoration.

DUNGENESS CRAB CAKE,
RADISH AND WASABI AIOLI, ASIAN SLAW
BY MARC LATULIPPE

This appetizer is a combination of hot and cold preparation; the cold side can be prepped ahead of time and the crab cakes seared and cooked just before serving for optimum freshness.

MARC LATULIPPE

I live with Marina my wife of 22 years, together with our pets — two dogs and three cats.

I am originally from Montréal, but before moving to the Maritimes we lived on the Canadian west coast for many years. Our house is situated on two acres of farm land with a huge organic garden and we also raise heirloom Chantecler chickens.

I love this at-home dish because of its simplicity; it's so easy to prepare. I like any ingredient that is fresh, local and in season. It's especially good if it comes from our own garden or picked in the wild! My favorite hobby is hiking with my dogs in the forest hunting for chanterelles and other wild edibles.

"I like any ingredient that is fresh, local and in season"

DUNGENESS CRAB CAKE,
RADISH AND WASABI AIOLI, ASIAN SLAW
BY MARC LATULIPPE

serves 4

ingredients

radish and wasabi aioli:

2	egg yolks
1 tsp	wasabi paste
¼ cup	sesame seed oil
1 cup	grapeseed oil
1 tsp	rice vinegar
2 tsp	soy sauce
2	radishes, chopped very fine or grated

Asian slaw:

2 cups	Napa cabbage, sliced fine
½ cup	carrots, fine julienne
2 tsp	scallions, sliced fine
2 tbsp	soy sauce
4 tbsp	sesame seed oil
2 tbsp	rice vinegar

crab cakes:

8½ oz	fresh crabmeat
2 tbsp	red pepper, fine dice
1 tsp	cilantro, chopped fine
1 tsp	scallion, sliced fine
1 oz	mayonnaise
1	egg white
salt & pepper, to taste	

method

radish and wasabi aioli:

Proceed as for a mayonnaise: emulsify the yolks and wasabi, add the oils gradually while whisking constantly; finish with the rest of the ingredients.

Asian slaw:

Mix all the ingredients together 2 hours before serving, and allow to marinate in the refrigerator.

crab cakes:

Have all the ingredients ready. Just before serving combine all the ingredients and shape into four round patties. Carefully sear on both sides in a hot pan, then place on a baking tray and cook in the oven for 5 minutes at 375°F.

to serve:

Drain the slaw and place on plates, top each with a crab cake, and drizzle with the aioli; add your favorite garnish and voilà … enjoy!

POACHED FARM EGGS,
GRITS COOKED IN RAW SHEEP'S MILK, AND TENNESSEE BLACK TRUFFLE

BY ADAM COOKE

This is a simple first course with a very restorative nature. As with most simple dishes, the quality of all of your ingredients is non-negotiable ... they must be the best. Serve this dish in the Winter when the best black truffles are available.

ADAM COOKE

I was born in California, grew up in Montana and went to culinary school in Vermont. I live in east Tennessee with my wife Bailey and daughter, Juniper.

This dish is a favorite of mine because it involves only ingredients from our area - local truffles, our hand-milled grits, our farm fresh eggs and our sheep's milk cheeses.

My hobbies are going fly-fishing and cycling as well as playing the guitar and banjo. My favorite ingredient? It's too hard to pick just one!

POACHED FARM EGGS,
GRITS COOKED IN RAW SHEEP'S MILK, AND TENNESSEE BLACK TRUFFLE

BY ADAM COOKE

serves 4

ingredients

5 cups	fresh sheep's milk or whole milk
2 cups	stoneground white grits
1 lb	aged Blackberry Farm Singing Brook cheese or pecorino

kosher salt

4	large eggs, fresh

sea salt & black pepper

1	large truffle, fresh

spring onions, green part only, chopped

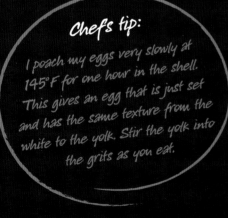

Chefs tip:

I poach my eggs very slowly at 145°F for one hour in the shell. This gives an egg that is just set and has the same texture from the white to the yolk. Stir the yolk into the grits as you eat.

method

grits:

Bring the milk to a simmer and season lightly. Whisk in your grits and lower the heat to the lowest setting on your stove. Cover with a lid and stir occasionally to ensure the grits don't stick. If your lowest setting is still too high then move your heatproof pot to a 300°F oven. In either case cook for about 3 hours until the grits are very soft and creamy. Stir in more milk during the cooking process if the grits look a little dry. Finish with some grated cheese and correct the seasoning. Keep covered until ready to serve.

eggs:

Bring a medium-size pot of water slowly up to temperature using a reliable thermometer. Add your eggs and keep checking the temperature to ensure that it remains constant. Hold at room temperature if you are not ready to serve but try to time the cooking with your grits so everything is ready at once.

to serve:

Stir the grits and ensure that they are soft and luxurious, then spoon into four small bowls, keeping in mind that they will 'set' slightly as they rest. I serve mine a little on the loose side to ensure the correct texture at the table. Using a spoon gently crack your eggs in a circle around the wider end of the egg and let

DUNGENESS CRAB SALAD
AVOCADO PUREE, MICRO HERBS, SUMMER MELONS, CREME FRAICHE VINAIGRETTE

BY MATTHEW STOWE

We get amazing fresh crab at Sonora.
This is a tribute to Dane Campbell, our
crab fisherman. When we serve crab
salads at the resort I like the crab to really
be the main focal point. In this recipe
I have added avocado purée for a little
richness and mouth watering feel. The
melon gives the dish a nice crispy texture
and the crème fraiche vinaigrette gives the
salad some structure without it masking the
true flavor of the Dungeness crab.

MATTHEW STOWE

I am newly wedded to my wife Amber and together we have a pug puppy named Ruby. We have just bought a house in my hometown of Cloverdale, British Columbia, before that we were living in downtown Vancouver. Most of my childhood was in Cloverdale and once I turned 18 I moved to New York to go to cooking school at the Culinary Institute of America.

I chose this home dish because all the ingredients can be found in a grocery store and there aren't any techniques that would intimidate any home cooks. My favorite ingredient would be our local spot prawns, they are so sweet and they freeze very well which is great because they have a very short season. I love sports, especially playing ice hockey, soccer as well as watching my beloved NFL football team The Seattle Seahawks. I also enjoy going to the park with my wife and our puppy Ruby.

"all the ingredients can be found in a gro

DUNGENESS CRAB SALAD,
AVOCADO PUREE, MICRO HERBS, SUMMER MELONS, CREME FRAICHE VINAIGRETTE

BY MATTHEW STOWE

serves 4

ingredients

crab mix:

¾ lb	picked Dungeness crab meat
2 tbsp	crème fraîche vinaigrette (see below)
3 tbsp	cucumber peeled, seeded and cut into brunoise
3 tbsp	celery brunoise
2 tbsp	finely cut chives

avocado purée:

2	ripe avocados
1½ tsp	lime juice
pinch of espelette pepper	
salt, to taste	

crème fraîche vinaigrette:

¼ cup	crème fraîche
1	lemon zested with a microplane and juiced
2 tbsp	olive oil
salt & pepper, to taste	

to serve:

½ cup	watermelon, cut into small dice
20	parisienne scoop balls of honeydew melon
6	squash blossoms, torn into small pieces
micro herbs or small chervil sprigs	

method

crab mix:

Place the crab, 2 tablespoons of the vinaigrette, cucumber, celery and the chives in a medium mixing bowl and fold everything together until well mixed.

avocado purée:

Cut the avocados in half and remove the pits; using a spoon scoop out all the avocado flesh. Place the avocado, lime juice, salt and pepper in a food processor and blend until smooth. Place in a plastic container and refrigerate until ready to use.

crème fraîche vinaigrette:

Combine all the ingredients in a small mixing bowl and whisk until well incorporated. Set aside.

to serve:

Place a spoon of the avocado purée on one end of the plate then, using a small spatula, spread the purée across the plate. Place a rectangular or circular ring mold in the center of each plate. Divide the crab mixture into the molds and pack the mixture well using the back of the spoon. Carefully lift off the molds. Spoon some of the vinaigrette around the plate, garnish with the watermelon dice, five honeydew balls per plate, and a few pieces of the micro herbs and squash blossoms. Serve immediately.

BUTTERNUT SQUASH SOUP,
ROASTED PUMPKIN SEEDS AND OIL

BY ANNE DESJARDINS AND
EMMANUEL R. DESJARDINS

A very easy, lazy Fall recipe, full of flavors, each adding to the other.

ANNE DESJARDINS

> "squash gives such an intense, sweet flavor"

I was born and raised in Montréal and met my partner Pierre Audette while studying at University. I have two children; Emmanuel and Félix and I'm now a grandmother as Emmanuel has a son called William. We used to live upstairs from our restaurant and lived there for 15 years but now we live near the woods just 10 minutes away from the restaurant in Val David. In my spare time I like to paint and some of my work is displayed on the walls of the restaurant and hotel.

I have chosen the butternut squash soup because I love soup, it's so easy that even a less confident cook can make it. Plus squash gives such an intense, sweet flavor and it makes a lovely color — really vivid! I ensure that I use fresh seasonal ingredients and I have a favorite for each season. Springtime it's lobster, Summer, wild blueberries and in Fall/Winter venison. And of course all year round the famous Québec's artisans' duck foie gras and cheeses.

BUTTERNUT SQUASH SOUP,
ROASTED PUMPKIN SEEDS AND OIL

BY ANNE DESJARDINS AND EMMANUEL R. DESJARDINS

serves 6

ingredients

butternut soup:

1 lb   fresh butternut squash
1   medium onion, peeled
2   cloves of garlic, peeled
2 tbsp   vegetable oil (canola or olive oil)
2-3 cups chicken broth
½ tsp   organic apple cider vinegar or lemon
          juice
salt, to taste
drops of Tabasco

to serve:

2 tbsp   pumpkin seeds, roasted
drops of pumpkin seed oil
drops of yogurt

method

butternut soup:

Preheat the oven to 425°F.

Line a sheet pan with aluminum foil.

Cut the butternut squash in half and remove the seeds. Place the squash on the pan, add the onion and garlic, and drizzle with oil. Cook for 45 minutes, until cooked and golden brown. Remove from the oven and let it cool a bit. Then, with a spoon, scoop the cooked flesh out of the squash. Put in the bowl of the blender with the onion and garlic. Add 1 cup of broth and blend well. Then pour this in to a pot over a medium heat. Add the remaining broth, whisk gently until hot. Season with apple cider vinegar (or lemon juice), salt, and Tabasco to taste.

to serve:

Pour the soup into hot soup bowls, garnish with roasted pumpkin seeds, oil and yogurt.

Chefs tip:
If the soup is too thick for your liking dilute with more broth. If you don't like pumpkin oil just skip that item.

GARLIC BUTTER BAKED QUADRA ISLAND OYSTERS

BY JOHN WALLER

Have you heard of the Clayoquot Oyster Festival? There is a reason we are so well known for these sustainable bi-valves. This simple, uncomplicated recipe is easy to prepare at home, and really showcases the true flavor of our amazing local oysters.

JOHN WALLER

I was born in London, England but have spent most of my life in Toronto, Ontario. Now I live in the Town of Tofino and have been here for over three years. I love this dish because it is so simple in its ingredients as well as preparation, and is such a great dish to share with friends. It's very hard to choose one favorite ingredient but water is very important. I love having a garden and growing plants especially those I can use in my cooking.

We try to source all our food directly from the producer and farmer and we try to form personal relationships with them; the oysters we use come from Outlandish Seafood Guild. They grow shellfish in the remote and wild outer islands of Discovery Islands and Desolation Sound, they are a group of the finest shellfish growers, operating eight individual family farms. They produce, market and personally deliver their fresh catch to us every week.

GARLIC BUTTER BAKED QUADRA ISLAND OYSTERS

BY JOHN WALLER

serves 2

ingredients

poached oysters:

6	oysters shucked – reserve juice

strained reserved juice and bottom shells

½ cup	Chenin Blanc wine
6	oyster shells cleaned and scrubbed

coarse salt for baking

garlic butter:

3 tbsp	lemon juice (juice from about 1 lemon)
3	shallots, finely chopped
3	cloves garlic, finely chopped
¼ cup	chopped Italian parsley (leaves only)
1 lb	unsalted butter, room temperature

pinch of salt & pepper

to serve:

Reggiano cheese
lemons

method

garlic butter:

Combine the lemon juice, shallots, garlic and chopped parsley with the butter until the ingredients are fully mixed. Spread out a large (1' or bigger) square of plastic wrap across your work surface, and then scoop the mixed butter onto the plastic. You are now going to roll the butter into a cylinder inside the plastic wrap. Tie the excess plastic wrap at the ends of the cylinder into a knot, or just use little pieces of string to tie off the ends. You can even make a string out of a short section of plastic wrap and roll it into a little rope. Refrigerate until needed.

poached oysters:

Bring the wine and reserved juice to a gentle simmer, add the oysters and remove from the heat. Let sit for 1 minute and remove, placing the oysters back into cleaned oyster shells.

final assembly and to serve:

Preheat the oven to 400°F. Cover a small baking pan with coarse salt, this will serve as a base to keep the oysters from moving during baking. Place the oysters, in shells, on salt in an oven proof dish. Take a slice of garlic butter about the size of a loonie (Canadian one dollar coin), place on top of each oyster and bake until the butter is completely melted (approximately 10 minutes). Remove from the oven and grate Reggiano on each oyster. Serve with lemon and enjoy.

Chef's tip:

During the Summer BBQ season the oysters can be placed on the grill, flat side up till they pop open. Then just remove the top and place the garlic butter on top.

'RAW AND COOKED' VEGETABLE SALAD

BY DAMON GORDON

The Raw and Cooked Vegetable Salad
is a salad for all seasons using all and
whatever vegetables are in season.
That is what makes this dish such a
go-to favorite of mine.

DAMON GORDON

I have one daughter who is 10 months old and her name is Riley Ella – she is my true angel. We live in Washington DC, within walking distance of the hotel and restaurant. Originally I am from Ipswich, Suffolk, England and I am the son of an English mother and Guyanese father.

I have chosen this recipe as my at-home dish because I love vegetables and this is a very healthy dish that is suitable for all seasons. My favorite ingredient is salt, it's a necessity in cooking. My hobbies are studying Muay Thai, a martial art from Thailand and riding my motorcycle.

"a very healthy dish that is suitable for all seasons"

'RAW AND COOKED' VEGETABLE SALAD

BY DAMON GORDON

serves 4

ingredients

5	baby red beets
5	baby golden beets
5	baby striped beets
6	sprigs of fresh thyme
10	baby orange carrots
10	baby yellow carrots
6	baby fennel
3	cloves garlic, peeled
vegetable stock or water	
8	asparagus spears, tips and stalks
1	medium shallot, minced
¼ cup	Champagne vinegar
1 cup	extra virgin olive oil + extra for drizzling
salt & pepper	
1	head frisée salad (cleaned)
¼	bunch fine chives, chopped
¼	bunch chervil
1 pt	mache salad (cleaned)

method

Preheat the oven to 375ºF. Wash the beets and pat dry. Place four beets of one color in foil, season, add a sprig of thyme and drizzle with olive oil. Repeat the process with the other beets. Enclose the foil and roast for 30-40 minutes until tender. Allow to cool, peel off the skin with a damp cloth, and quarter.

In three separate pans place eight orange carrots, eight yellow carrots and four baby fennel. Season each pan, add a sprig of thyme, a half clove of garlic and cover with either water or stock until they are just submerged. Cook until tender over a moderate heat. Place on a perforated tray in the refrigerator to cool down.

Cut the asparagus stalks into a fine dice and sauté quickly with the shallot and one clove of smashed garlic. Once tender, place this 'marmalade' flat on a small tray and refrigerate.

Make a vinaigrette by combining the vinegar and olive oil and season. Set aside.

Slice the remaining raw vegetables lengthways as thinly as possible and place in iced water for 15 minutes.

to serve:

Season the cooked vegetables with salt and pepper, chives and some vinaigrette. Place equal amounts of the 'marmalade' in the center of the plates and arrange the cooked vegetables around it. Mix the shaved vegetables with the frisée, chives, chervil and season with salt, pepper and three spoons of vinaigrette. Place on top. Finish with mache salad mixed with one to two spoons of vinaigrette.

Chef's tip:

For a 'shaved' effect slice the raw vegetables lengthways as thinly as possible.

BUTTERNUT SQUASH VELOUTE,
BACON, CROSTINIS AND CHIVE CREAM

**BY JOACHIM SPLICHAL
AND TONY ESNAULT**

*This easy-to-prepare dish is a favorite
with Patina's guests. A perfect starter
for your next dinner party that will leave
your guests asking for more!*

JOACHIM SPLICHAL

I have twin sons named Nicolas and Stephane, together we love entertaining our family and friends in our San Marino home on weekends and holidays. The Butternut Squash Velouté that I have chosen for my at-home dish is really popular with Patina guests and it's so easy to prepare.

My favorite ingredients have to be vegetables, organically grown, and steak. In my spare time I enjoy activities such as skiing and playing tennis. I also enjoy collecting wines and contemporary art. I'm building up quite a collection!

Chef's tip:
You can make the croutons and the bacon lardons ahead to save time.

BUTTERNUT SQUASH VELOUTE,
BACON, CROSTINIS AND CHIVE CREAM

BY JOACHIM SPLICHAL AND TONY ESNAULT

serves 4

ingredients

velouté:

⅛ lb	butter, unsalted
1	thick slice of bacon
2	garlic cloves
2	butternut squashes, peeled and diced small
½ cup	heavy cream
½ cup	whole milk
4 cups	chicken stock
salt & freshly ground black pepper	

garnish:

1 tbsp	clarified butter
4	slices white bread, medium diced
3	slices bacon, small dice
1 tsp	chives, chopped
¼ cup	whipped cream
salt & freshly ground black pepper	

method

velouté:

In a large pot, melt the butter and add the bacon and garlic. Sweat the bacon and add the butternut squash. Add salt and stir. Keeping on a low heat, continue to stir the squash until very dry and cooked all of the way. Once completely dry and cooked, add the heavy cream and stir, then add the milk and chicken stock. Combine well and bring to a boil. Add salt and pepper, remove the bacon and purée in a blender. Pass through a chinois.

garnish:

In a hot pan, melt the clarified butter and toss the cut bread in the butter until golden brown. Remove, strain the butter out and dry the crostinis on paper towels. In a separate hot pan, render the bacon until golden and crispy. Let the bacon dry over paper towels and set aside. For the chive cream, fold the chopped chives into the whipped cream and season. Keep the chive cream cold until you are ready to serve.

to serve:

Re-heat the soup and adjust the seasoning. Pour into four hot soup bowls. Sprinkle the crostinis and bacon on top of the soup. Place a spoonful of the chive cream in the middle of the plate and serve immediately.

RICOTTA GNOCCHI
WITH TRUFFLED CREME FRAICHE AND BABY TOMATOES

BY JASON ROBINSON

*Homemade ricotta gnocchi
with organic baby tomatoes
for a splash of color.*

JASON ROBINSON

Originally I come from Ann Arbor, Michigan but I grew up in southern California. Now I live in Cypress, Texas just outside of Houston with my daughter, Lucynda Rose. I have chosen this at-home dish because it's one of our customers' favorites and I want to share it with them so they can make it at home.

My favorite ingredient is just pork in general, whether it is bacon, chops or smoked jowls - I love it. When I have time I like to garden with my daughter. It's nice to spend time together outside.

"one of our customers' favorites"

RICOTTA GNOCCHI
WITH TRUFFLED CREME FRAICHE AND BABY TOMATOES

BY JASON ROBINSON

serves 4-6

ingredients

½ lb	ricotta cheese, drained
⅓ lb	parmesan cheese, grated
4 tbsp	truffle oil
1	egg
2¼ cups	all purpose flour
⅓ cup	crème fraîche
1 tbsp	heavy cream
1 tbsp	black truffle, chopped
12	sweet cherry tomatoes, halved

salt & pepper, to taste
micro arugula, for garnish

method

One hour before preparation, drain the ricotta over cheesecloth.

In a large mixing bowl, combine the drained ricotta, parmesan cheese, truffle oil, and egg. Slowly incorporate the flour until everything is evenly combined, then let the dough rest in the refrigerator for 1 hour. Remove the chilled dough and lightly flour the work surface. Roll the dough into a rope 1″ thick in diameter, then cut into 1″ pieces. Shape each piece into a ball and then roll on the tines of a fork to create grooves.

Set a pot of water on the stove and bring to a boil. In the meantime, prepare the sauce by heating the crème fraîche with the cream and truffles in a pan over a medium heat. Let it reduce down until the desired thickness. Season to taste.

to serve:

Place the gnocchi in the boiling water (do not crowd the pot) and allow to cook until they float to the surface. Remove the cooked gnocchi from the water and transfer to the sauce. Add the tomatoes, check for seasoning and finish with the micro arugula.

BLT

BY NORMAND LAPRISE

*A really versatile dish – this unique take
on a classic is perfect at any time of year.*

NORMAND LAPRISE

I have three children, my son Thomas and my two daughters Béatrice and the youngest of the family, Juliette. I currently live in Montréal but I was born in Kamouraska in Canada. It's in the country near the St-Laurent river.

I chose the BLT because you can adapt the kind of tomatoes you use depending on the month; it is especially good in August or September. You can also change the kind of herbs you use, depending on what you like. It's really a seasonal dish, and a tomato in season is so good!

My favorite ingredients are rhubarb, tarragon, razor clams, white asparagus and snow crab, having any of these in a dish is great. My hobbies are golf, travel and I also have an interest in Japanese knives – they're always beautifully made.

"it's really a seasonal dish, and a tomato in season is so good"

BLT

BY NORMAND LAPRISE

serves 4

ingredients

4	medium-sized ripe tomatoes
12	slices of pancetta
4 tbsp	'fried bread'
peanut oil, for frying	
4 tbsp	Chardonnay vinegar
6 tbsp	extra virgin olive oil
salt & freshly ground pepper	
4 tbsp	shallots, finely minced
1 cup	homemade mayonnaise
basil leaves	
lettuce leaves	
chives, cut into 1½" lengths	
4 tbsp	parmesan finely grated
mayonnaise, to taste	

method

Preheat the oven to 325°F.

Blanch and peel the tomatoes and remove the core using a large apple corer.

Place the slices of pancetta in between two sheets of parchment paper and put on a baking sheet. Cook in the oven for about 20-30 minutes or until golden brown and crisp.

For the 'fried bread' grind croutons in a mixer. Strain through a fine sieve to remove the fine powder, leaving chunkier crumbs. Heat a pot of oil to 380°F. Using the sieve as a fryer basket, fry the crumbs for about 1-2 minutes until golden brown. Remove immediately and place on a paper towel to drain.

to serve:

Take a sliver off the bottom of each tomato and then slice horizontally into four equal slices. Lay the slices on a tray keeping the respective slices next to each other (it makes it much easier when it`s time to re-stack the slices to make the tomato whole again!). Drizzle all the slices liberally with Chardonnay vinegar, extra virgin olive oil and season well with salt and pepper. Sprinkle the tomato slices with the shallots. Then place two small dollops of mayonnaise on each slice and follow by layering a few basil leaves, some lettuce leaves, a few chives, and then sprinkle some parmesan and fried bread on each. Finish by placing 1 slice of pancetta on each layer and very carefully replace the slices on top of each other to reassemble the tomato. Spoon a little bit of mayonnaise on top, drizzle with olive oil and sprinkle with salt.

POTATO SALAD

**BY VAUGHN PERRET
AND CHARLES LEARY**

*The pinks and purples in this dish make
it a great dish to look at as well as to eat!*

VAUGHN PERRET AND CHARLES LEARY

We split our time between manning the stoves at Trout Point in Nova Scotia and a home in Granada, Spain. A native of New Orleans, Vaughn grew up inspired by festive Creole-style Sunday dinners at his grandmother's house. Charles was born in Oregon and developed an early appreciation of the movement to develop local food and wine on the U.S. west coast. Our heirloom potato salad is perfect for the home cook, being a twist on a tried and true favorite, and easily adapatable to local ingredients. We both enjoy photography and finding new culinary inspiration through travel, which has included China, Central America, India, as well as Western Europe.

"a twist on a tried and true favorite "

Chef's tip:

Watch the cooking of the purple potatoes very carefully so as not to overcook them: they will become grainy and lose color.

POTATO SALAD

BY VAUGHN PERRET AND CHARLES LEARY

serves 4

ingredients

3	medium purple potatoes, peeled and cubed
3	medium pink potatoes, peeled and cubed
4 tbsp	extra virgin olive oil
½ tbsp	balsamic vinegar
½ tbsp	fresh lemon juice
½	lemon, zest
1 tbsp	fresh parsley, roughly chopped
¼ tsp	fresh rosemary, chopped
1 tsp	very coarsely ground or crushed black peppercorns
¼ lb	baby Gulf of Maine shrimps, or other small shrimps, cooked

method

Bring water to a boil in a large saucepan. Boil the large cubes of purple potatoes for 4 minutes. Boil the pink potatoes for 6 minutes. Drain, and allow to cool and dry.

In a large glass or stainless steel bowl add the remaining ingredients except for the shrimps. When the potatoes are cool and dry, toss into the seasoning mixture, let sit for 15 minutes, add the shrimps, and toss again. Let sit again for 15 minutes.

to serve:

Toss all the ingredients together then serve.

The falafel can be eaten hot right away, or made in advance and eaten cold over a salad, in a sandwich or simply as a snack.

FALAFEL
BY ELI KAIMEH

ELI KAIMEH

I come from Brooklyn in the
heart of New York City. I
have been at Per Se since
the restaurant first opened in
2004. Our goal is to craft
a daily menu which reflects
modern American cuisine with
a touch of French influence.
My favorite ingredient to use
in cooking is salt and I enjoy
reading cookbooks and eating
out on my days off.

I have chosen the falafel as
my at-home dish because it is
easily executed and versatile.
The main ingredients are a
combination of vegetables
and wheat, so it is also a
nutritious dish.

FALAFEL

BY ELI KAIMEH

serves 8

ingredients

falafel:

3 cups	chickpeas
½ cup + 1 tbsp	bulgur wheat
3	medium yellow onions, roughly chopped
15	cloves garlic, peeled
3 tbsp	cumin seeds, whole
3 tbsp	coriander seeds, whole
1 tbsp	black peppercorns, whole
1 tbsp	kosher salt, + more to taste
3 tbsp	mint, finely chopped
3 tbsp	cilantro, finely chopped
3 tbsp	parsley, finely chopped
3 tbsp	white sesame seeds
3 tbsp	baking soda
1-2 qt	canola oil

to serve:

hummus, raita and pita bread

method

falafel:

Place the chickpeas and bulgur wheat each in a bowl and add water to cover by 2". Cover and soak overnight.

Drain well and grind through the small die of a meat grinder into a large bowl. Grind the onions and garlic through the meat grinder into a bowl set under a fine-mesh strainer. Press on the onions to release the excess juice. Discard the juices, then add the onion mixture to the chickpea mixture.

In a small skillet over a medium heat, toast the cumin and coriander seeds until fragrant. Transfer to a spice grinder, add the peppercorns and grind into a powder. Transfer the spices to the chickpea mixture, along with the salt, mint, cilantro, parsley and sesame seeds. Stir to combine. Mix in the baking soda and let stand for 30 minutes. Season to taste with salt.

Heat a medium pot filled 2" with canola oil to 350ºF. Using your hands, shape the chickpea mixture into 2" balls. Fry in batches for 3 minutes or until dark brown and cooked through.

to serve:

Serve in pita bread with raita and hummus.

FISH &
CRUSTACEAN
MAIN DISHES

If seafood is your passion, these tantalizing recipes
are sure to inspire you. Explore locally available
seafood and celebrate the abundance of the fresh fish
of our rivers and oceans. Enter into the culinary
universe of top chefs and experience their love of the
sea and its produce.

With dishes such as Colin Bedford's 'Beet Cured Salmon'
the colors and flavors of this dish are certain to be a
talking point with guests and hosts alike. And for that
'wow factor!' see 'Sushi Pizza', one of Hotel Fauchère's
signature dishes selected by Christopher P. Bates.

STEAMED MANILA CLAMS,
GLAZED PORK BELLY, LIME, THAI BASIL
BY ROBERT CURRY

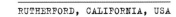

The shallots, white wine and fresh herbs are wonderfully balanced in this dish. Clams by themselves are excellent; however, the stand-out ingredient here is the glazed pork belly. The freshness of the basil makes this dish complex and exceptional.

ROBERT CURRY

When I'm not in the restaurant, I spend most of my free time with my wife and three children. When I am home, I cook, I play a lot of guitar - I started playing when I was 18 and never had any lessons but it's relaxing for me. As a kid I grew up going to the Sierras - I like to backpack and make my destination somewhere I can find mountain trout.

Produce has always driven my menu. Fruits and vegetables are the seasonality of how menus are created. The more I learned about cooking, the more I saw it was rooted in tradition. My fondest southern California food memory is eating home-cooked clams - a favorite childhood memory of mine. Clams and pork belly are a very rich dish yet, when prepared this way, they are both comforting and familiar. In all I would say that my favorite ingredient is bacon.

Chef's tip:
The pork belly and glaze can be prepared a day in advance.

STEAMED MANILA CLAMS,
GLAZED PORK BELLY, LIME, THAI BASIL

BY ROBERT CURRY

serves 4

ingredients

pork belly:

1¼ lb	fresh pork belly, skin removed
½ tsp	whole black peppercorns
1	whole star anise
½ tsp	whole cloves
½ tsp	fennel seeds
½ tsp	ground cinnamon
salt, to taste	
1	garlic head, halved
½	carrot, peeled and sliced
½	onion, peeled and medium dice
½	fennel bulb, medium dice
½	leek, medium dice
½	bunch of thyme, tied with butcher's twine
1	bay leaf
1½ cups	dry white wine
1½ qt	chicken stock
1 tbsp	grapeseed oil

pork belly glaze:

4 tbsp	brown sugar
¼ cup	soy sauce
¼ cup	mirin

clams:

2 tbsp	ginger, peeled and minced
1 tbsp	garlic, peeled and minced
2 tbsp	shallots, peeled and minced
2 tbsp	grapeseed oil
6 lb	Manila clams
1 cup	dry white wine
2 tbsp	sweet chili sauce
2 tbsp	Thai fish sauce
½ cup	lime juice

to serve:

2 oz	butter
24	Thai basil leaves, chiffonade
4	green onions, sliced

method

pork belly and glaze:

Preheat the oven to 300ºF. Score the fat on the skin side of the belly with a knife. Grind together the peppercorns, star anise, cloves, fennel seeds and cinnamon. In a small sauté pan toast the spices over a low heat for about a minute, then remove from the pan. Season the pork liberally with salt, then rub with the ground spice mix.

Heat a medium saucepot, and add the pork, fat side down. Sear the pork well on all sides, then remove from the pot. Add the garlic, carrot, onion, fennel, leek, thyme and bay leaf. Cook slowly until the vegetables are tender. Add the wine and reduce by half. Add the pork belly and chicken stock. Bring to a simmer and cover with a lid. Place in the oven for 2 hours. Remove from the oven and take the pork from the liquid. Place the pork between two sheet pans and place something heavy on top to weigh it down. Refrigerate for at least 6 hours. Once the pork is thoroughly chilled and pressed, portion into at least 12 large diced pieces. Reserve. To finish the pork, heat a sauté pan, add the grapeseed oil, then the pork, and sear on all sides. Remove excess fat from the pan and add the ingredients for the glaze. Reduce just until the pork is glazed.

clams:

In a large pot over a low heat sweat the ginger, garlic and shallots in the oil. Add the clams, wine, chili sauce, fish sauce, and lime juice. Cover with a lid, turn up the heat and steam open the clams.

to serve:

Divide the clams among four warm bowls. Whisk the butter into the cooking liquid from the clams. Ladle the liquid over the clams and place the glazed pork belly on top. Garnish with the basil and green onions.

NEW ENGLAND SEAFOOD NAGE
MUSSELS, LITTLENECKS, SCALLOPS, CIPOLLINI ONIONS, YUKON GOLD POTATOES, FENNEL, SAFFRON

BY JONATHAN CAMBRA

Gathering inspiration from New England's abundant seafood, the New England Seafood Nage features delicacies from Narragansett Bay, the Atlantic Ocean and Georges Bank, as well as vegetables hand-picked from local farms.

JONATHAN CAMBRA

I'm currently Executive Chef at Castle Hill Inn & Resort and I love using locally-purchased ingredients, and organic produce. I like to draw on my Portuguese roots and try to influence our cuisine with subtle mediterranean spices and influences. I am often involved with good causes and I like giving back to the community with benefits such as the Rhode Island Food Bank's Taste of Rhode Island Show, Farm Fresh Rhode Island, American Red Cross, Great Chefs of Rhode Island Star Chefs Series and Chefs for Cystic Fibrosis.

I chose this dish because it is representative of the bountiful seafood in New England, although my favorite ingredient is wild ramps. I live in Bristol with my wife Melanie, daughter Zoë, and son Cody. When not in the kitchen, I enjoy spending time with my family, cooking with my children, snowboarding, saltwater fishing, farming vegetables and playing the drums.

"I love using locally-purchased ingredients, and organic produce"

NEW ENGLAND SEAFOOD NAGE
MUSSELS, LITTLENECKS, SCALLOPS, CIPOLLINI ONIONS, YUKON GOLD POTATOES, FENNEL, SAFFRON

BY JONATHAN CAMBRA

serves 4

ingredients

seafood:

4	Georges Bank sea scallops, cleaned
12	littleneck clams, washed of all sand
1	cipollini onion, peeled, blanched and quartered
2	Yukon gold potatoes, peeled, medium diced and blanched
2	fennel bulbs, quartered, cored and thinly shaved
	white wine
12	mussels, washed and de-bearded
	parsley sprigs, to garnish

saffron nage:

2	leeks, chopped
2	fennel bulbs, chopped
4	celery stalks, chopped
	olive oil
1	sachet (thyme, peppercorn, bay leaf)
2 cups	white wine
1 cup	Pernod
2 qt	fish stock or clam juice
	saffron
½ qt	heavy cream

method

saffron nage:

Sweat the leeks, fennel, and celery in olive oil until tender, being careful to not brown the vegetables at all. Add the sachet. Deglaze with the wine and Pernod and reduce by half. Add the fish stock and reduce by half. Add a good size pinch of saffron. Add the heavy cream and simmer for 5 or so minutes. Remove from the heat and strain. Add another pinch of saffron to the final product after it is strained and while it is still hot.

seafood:

Season the scallops and sear on both sides in a sauté pan, then remove from the pan. Add the littleneck clams, cipollini onion, potatoes and fennel. Deglaze with a small amount of white wine and then add half a cup of the saffron nage, cover, and simmer over a medium heat. Once the littleneck clams begin to open, add the mussels, and return the scallops to the pan. Add more saffron nage, or a little fish stock if the nage is too thick. Cook until the clams and mussels are open, and the scallops are tender. Finish with a pinch of parsley.

to serve:

In a bowl, place the littleneck clams and mussels around the edge (three per person), put the potatoes, fennel, and onions in the center of the bowl. Place a scallop on top, and pour the nage around. Garnish with fresh parsley.

RAPPAHANNOCK RIVER OYSTER CHOWDER WITH SMOKY BACON

BY DEAN MAUPIN

There are few things more comforting on a cool Fall day than a warm cup of creamy oyster stew, so simple yet intriguing to prepare. The freshness of the oysters is absolutely paramount, settle for nothing less than straight from the sea.

DEAN MAUPIN

My culinary background started at a young age working with my grandfather at his fruit stand in Crozet, Virginia. At 17 I worked my way into the kitchen of the only fine restaurant in my town. Later I apprenticed at the Greenbrier Hotel, the oldest culinary apprenticeship in America. After a brief time cooking in Napa Valley, California, I returned to my home of Albemarle County to settle and start a family.

I have two children, Ellery and my newborn son, Grant.

I live in Albemarle County, Virginia. My hobbies are gardening, fishing and my family.

I have chosen this cook at-home dish because I am obsessed with Virginia oysters, and it's so perfectly simple to prepare. My favorite ingredient is artisanal cheese of any variety.

" I am obsessed with Virginia oysters, so perfectly simple to prepare "

RAPPAHANNOCK RIVER OYSTER CHOWDER WITH SMOKY BACON

BY DEAN MAUPIN

serves 6

ingredients

4 oz	butter
1 cup	yellow onions, small diced
½ cup	celery, small diced
½ cup	leeks, rinsed and small diced
1 cup	fennel bulb, small diced
1 cup	potatoes, small diced
3	garlic cloves, smashed and minced
1½ cups	white wine
4 cups	half and half
sea salt & ground black pepper	
18	fresh oysters scrubbed, shucked and removed from their shells
1	heaped tablespoon each chopped tarragon, parsley, and chives
squeeze of fresh lemon	

to serve:

6 oz	smoked bacon, cooked and diced

method

In a heavy gauge soup pot over a medium heat melt the butter then add the onions, celery, leeks, fennel, and potatoes and cook for 4-5 minutes until the vegetables are tender. Add the minced garlic and continue cooking for another 2 minutes, stirring often, making sure the vegetables do not brown. Add the white wine and reduce by half then add the half and half. At this point allow the chowder to reach a boil then reduce the heat to low and allow to simmer for 10 minutes.

Season with salt and pepper. When you are 5 minutes away from serving, simply add the oysters to the simmering stew and allow to gently poach for 3-4 minutes until just cooked. To finish, stir in the fresh herbs and a squeeze of fresh lemon.

to serve:

Ladle the chowder into the serving bowls and garnish with the smoky bacon.

COD LYONNAISE
BY DANIEL BOULUD

Tender white fish that pairs beautifully with crispy Lyonnaise potatoes. Easy and utterly delicious.

DANIEL BOULUD

I live in New York and have a daughter named Alix. I was born in St. Pierre de Chandieu, France, a small village near Lyon in the Rhône Valley. I would have to choose a few favorite ingredients for each season. In the Spring: peas and lettuce; in Summer: sweet corn and tomatoes; Fall: white truffle on a baked potato; Winter: a chicken roasted with black truffle under the skin.

In this recipe, I aimed for ease and flavor. I love the meatiness of cod, simply seared, skin side down. I serve it with potatoes Lyonnaise which are crispy, slightly tart from deglazing with sherry vinegar and just a little sweet, thanks to the onions.

"I love the meatiness of cod, simply seared, skin side down"

COD LYONNAISE

BY DANIEL BOULUD

serves 4

ingredients

seared cod:

4	center-cut cod fillets, skin left on, 6 oz each
1 tbsp	extra virgin olive oil
	salt & freshly ground pepper
4	cloves garlic, lightly crushed
4	sprigs of thyme
1 tbsp	unsalted butter

potatoes Lyonnaise:

3 tbsp	extra virgin olive oil
1½ lb	Yukon Gold potatoes, peeled and cut into ½" dice
1½ lb	sweet onions, cut into ½" dice
	salt & freshly ground pepper
2 tbsp	sherry vinegar

to serve:

6	sprigs of flat-leaf parsley leaves, sliced

method

seared cod:

Warm the olive oil in a large skillet over a medium-high heat. Season the fillets with salt and pepper and slip them into the pan, skin side down, along with the garlic and thyme. Sear for 3 minutes, turn them over and cook for 3 minutes more. Reduce the heat to medium, add the butter and cook for another 3 minutes, or until the fish is opaque, moist, and lightly firm when pressed. Serve immediately.

potatoes Lyonnaise:

Warm the olive oil in a large non-stick skillet over a medium-high heat. Add the potatoes and cook, while tossing, for 10 minutes. Add the onions, season with salt and pepper, and cook until the onions are translucent and the potatoes tender, about 5-10 minutes. Pour in the vinegar and cook until it has reduced to a glaze.

to serve:

Spoon the potatoes onto a serving platter, top with the seared cod, and sprinkle with the parsley.

SUSHI PIZZA
BY HOTEL FAUCHERE

*A long-standing staple at the Hotel
Fauchère, the Sushi Pizza has acted as
a signature dish since day one in our
Bar Louis. Chef Michael Glatz, the chef
involved in the reopening of the Hotel
Fauchère, brought this dish with him and
has left it behind as a part of his legacy.
We have chosen this as our 'do at-home'
recipe, not because it can be tossed
together in a flash, but rather because
like sushi, once the prep work is done,
it can hold and be finished and served
quickly. Ideal for a dinner party.*

CHRISTOPHER P. BATES

I currently live about a mile away from the restaurant near a beautiful stream called the Sawkill, although originally I am from Arkport, New York, a small town quite far away from the lights of New York City! My at-home dish was actually created by the first chef at the restaurant, Michael Glatz, and it is a dish that the hotel has become somewhat famous for. The best thing about it is that most of the preparation of this dish can be done in advance but still wows guests - plus it's easy to make!

My favorite ingredients change with the seasons but wild indigenous ingredients really excite me, to taste things that people living on this land hundreds of years ago tasted. Also humble ingredients; I am a big fan of products less appreciated such as mackerel and sardines, even classic staples like tomatoes. In my spare time I have begun writing about wine, and I am continuing to study for my Master Sommelier exam. Outside the world of food and drink I enjoy fly fishing, photography and sunshine.

Chef's tip:
Try to add the seasoned vinegar with a portable fan blowing into the bowl, or someone fanning with a piece of cardboard.

SUSHI PIZZA

BY HOTEL FAUCHERE

serves 4-6

ingredients

sushi rice:

1 cup	sushi rice
1 cup	cold water
1 tbsp	rice wine vinegar
1 tbsp	sugar
pinch of salt	

sauce:

¼ cup	orange tobiko caviar
1 cup	mayonnaise
1 tbsp	sriracha
1 tsp	cayenne pepper
4 tsp	soy sauce
1 oz	rice wine vinegar
1 oz	mirin
1 tbsp	fish sauce

scallion curls:

| 1 | bunch scallions |

tempura batter:

1	egg yolk
1 cup	club soda, ice cold
1 oz	sake, ice cold
1 cup	rice flour

tuna dice:

| ½ lb | sushi grade yellowfin or big eye tuna, ½" dice, refrigerated immediately, covered with a damp paper towel and then wrapped in plastic wrap. |

to serve:

oil for frying	
¼ cup	orange tobiko caviar
¼ cup	green tobiko caviar

Chefs tip:

Everything can be prepared 1 day in advance with the exception of the tempura batter and the tuna dice.

method

sushi rice:

Rinse the rice thoroughly under cold running water until the water runs clear. Place the rice and water in a heavy-bottomed pan. Over a medium-high heat, bring to a boil uncovered, then cover and turn down to medium-low for 10 minutes, then down to low for 15 minutes. Turn the heat off and allow the rice to rest covered and untouched for 20 minutes. Mix the vinegar, sugar and salt in a small pan and heat until dissolved. Put the rice into a wooden bowl. Add the seasoned vinegar and fold with a wooden rice paddle, being careful not to mash or break the rice, until it absorbs the seasoning, and becomes sticky and shiny, about 10 minutes. Using a ring mold and working on waxed paper or parchment on a tray form four to six circles about 5" x ½" high. Place the tray in the freezer.

sauce:

In a large bowl, mix all of the ingredients together, wrap tightly and chill in the refrigerator.

scallion curls:

Cut the green part only into long thin strips on an extreme bias, yielding scallion 'rings' ½"- 1" long. Stop when you hit the white part. Submerge in iced water and store in the refrigerator for up to 12 hours. The scallions should crisp up and begin to curl dramatically.

tempura batter:

Combine the wet ingredients. Whisk as you pour this mix into the flour until evenly blended and most lumps gone – about 20 seconds.

to serve:

Heat the oil to 365°F in a deep fryer or pan. Remove the rice circles from the freezer and dip into the tempura batter and then into the oil. Turning once or twice, fry until crispy and brown, around 3 minutes. Remove with a slotted spoon to a tray lined with paper towels. Keep warm in the oven. When all of the circles have been fried, cut each into 4-6 slices. Spoon sauce onto each disc and spread evenly with the back of a spoon. Sprinkle with tuna and caviar. Garnish with scallions.

"wonderful flavor, locally sourced and hard to beat"

This dish was designed for visual as well as flavor impact. 'The first bite is with your eyes' and the follow-through with the first bite proves that the fresh ingredient combinations do not fall short of flavor expectations.

BEET CURED SALMON,
LEMON AND CELERY ROOT CHUTNEY, CAPER
AND JASMINE RAISIN PUREE, FENNEL SALAD
BY COLIN BEDFORD

COLIN BEDFORD

I am a native of England and began my career at the Castle Hotel in Taunton as Commis Chef. In pursuit of my desire to see other cultures and experiences, I moved to Niagara on The Lake, Canada and worked at the Prince of Wales Hotel. In 2005 I became Executive Sous Chef at Fearrington and then became Executive Chef at the house restaurant in 2008.

My passion outside of the kitchen is outdoor sports and, in particular, I love the challenge of golf. My favorite ingredients to work with are fresh and unusual vegetables as well as custom grown organic micro greens that I obtain from my collaboration with Anne Stump, the farmer of the local Duckwood Farms in Pittsboro. I love creating new twists on old favorites and comfort foods.

Why this recipe? Salmon is readily available and a favorite with most home cooks. Curing with beet juice is a different approach that creates a wonderful and impressive color contrast and is easy to prepare in advance for a dinner party. The visual effect is amazing.

Chefs tip:
The salmon can be cured up to 24 hours in advance.

BEET CURED SALMON,
LEMON AND CELERY ROOT CHUTNEY, CAPER AND JASMINE RAISIN PUREE, FENNEL SALAD

BY COLIN BEDFORD

serves 12

ingredients

beet cure:

4 cups	sugar
2 cups	salt
¼ cup	cracked black pepper
3	pieces crushed star anise
4 tbsp	crushed coriander seeds
2 cups	beet juice
4 oz	dill, chopped
2	limes, zested
1	side of salmon

lemon and celery root chutney:

3	lemons, zest julienned and lemons segmented
3 cups	simple syrup
2	shallots, small diced
2	cardamom pods
1	celery root, medium diced

caper and jasmine raisin purée:

4 cups	water
2 oz	jasmine tea
3 cups	golden raisins
1 cup	capers

fennel salad:

2	bulbs of fennel, thinly shaved
salt	
1 tsp	dill, chopped
½	orange, juice
1 tsp	honey
¼ cup	olive oil

pickled mushrooms:

8 oz	Maitake mushrooms
1 cup	water
1 cup	Champagne vinegar
1 cup	sugar
1	shallot
2 oz	tarragon
1 tbsp	mustard seeds
1	piece star anise

to serve:

caviar and micro greens

method

beet cure:

Combine all the dry ingredients. Add the beet juice and mix until incorporated. Add the dill and zest. Pour into a container the same size as the salmon, place the salmon skin side up and cure for up to 24 hours. Wash and dry on paper towels and slice thinly just before serving.

lemon and celery root chutney:

Blanch the zest three times starting from cold water and refresh each time. Cover with syrup and cook until tacky. Sweat off the shallots without any color and add cardamom to infuse. Roast off the celery root in another pan until the edges start to turn brown then add to the shallots. Leave to cool and combine with the zest and segments. Season and adjust with additional syrup.

caper and jasmine raisin purée:

Boil the water and add the tea to infuse. Cool, re-boil and strain over the raisins and capers, then allow to cool. Remove from the water, place in a blender and gradually re-add water to make a thick purée. Strain.

fennel salad:

Sprinkle the fennel with salt and set aside for 45 minutes. Squeeze any additional moisture from the fennel using a cloth and combine with all other ingredients.

pickled mushrooms:

Apart from the mushrooms combine all other ingredients and boil. Sauté the mushrooms and deglaze with the pickling liquid.

to serve:

Place the fennel salad down the center of the plate and arrange the salmon on top. Arrange chutney and mushrooms alternately around the salmon. Dot the purée randomly around and garnish with micro greens, and caviar.

OYSTERS ROCKEFELLER

BY CHAD MARTIN

New Orleans and Louisiana, our Proprietor's home state, has a profound influence on the cuisine in our dining room. Oysters Rockefeller, a recipe invented and famous in New Orleans, is always available here.

CHAD MARTIN

I have a son named Jackson and we live in a small neighborhood in Dallas across from White Rock Lake called Little Forest Hills. I am a lifelong native of Dallas, Texas and enjoy living in the 'Lone Star State'. My favorite ingredient is olive oil and my hobbies are fishing, entertaining at home, boating and spending time with my family and friends.

I have chosen Oysters Rockefeller as my favorite dish to cook at home because it is unique and always well received by guests due to its presentation, well chosen ingredients and richness. It's also a perfect dish to serve when entertaining.

Chef's tip:

Purchase the oysters on the day of preparation. Serve on rock salt, seaweed, or a small mound of mashed potatoes to keep them stable.

OYSTERS ROCKEFELLER
BY CHAD MARTIN

serves 4

ingredients

12	fresh oysters, shucked

spinach and herb topping:

1 tbsp	canola oil
12 cups	fresh spinach
1	smoked bacon strip, small diced
3	shallots, minced
3	garlic cloves, minced
½	celery rib, peeled and diced
⅛ cup	Pernod or white wine (optional)
1½ cups	heavy cream
⅓ cup	Parmigiano Reggiano, grated
½ cup	Panko breadcrumbs
2 tbsp	parsley, chervil, tarragon, finely chopped
1 tsp	Worcestershire sauce

dash of Tabasco or other hot sauce
salt & pepper

to serve:

micro grated parmesan, shaved black or white truffle, béarnaise sauce, truffle oil (all optional)

method

Preheat the oven to 350°F. Heat the canola oil in a large skillet and sauté the spinach until wilted, then remove from the pan and cool. Chop roughly. Add the bacon to the hot pan and cook over a medium-high heat until almost crispy. Add the shallots, garlic and celery and sauté until translucent. Immediately add the Pernod or wine if using (stand away) and flame until the fire subsides while shaking the pan briskly. Add the heavy cream and cook until reduced by half. Turn off the heat and stir in the Parmigiano Reggiano, spinach, breadcrumbs, herbs, Worcestershire sauce and Tabasco. Season and cool to room temperature. Place a heaped portion of the spinach-herb mixture atop each oyster and bake in the oven until lightly toasted.

to serve:

Garnish as desired.

KENNEBUNKPORT LOBSTER
ON BRAISED LENTILS
AND ROSE BUTTER SAUCE

BY JONATHAN CARTWRIGHT

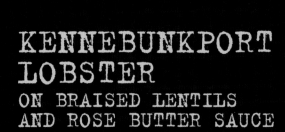

This is a simple and tasty dish that can easily be cooked on a grill at a Summer cookout.

JONATHAN CARTWRIGHT

I come from Sheffield in England
and I moved to the USA in 1993
to work at Blantyre in Lenox
Massachusetts and the Horned
Dorset Primavera in Puerto Rico
before moving to Kennebunkport
and The White Barn Inn in
April 1995. I have two young
daughters who were born in Maine
and attend the local school.
Kennebunkport has an abundance
of fresh seasonal seafood to
choose from for menu inspiration
while Maine's farmers are some
of the best in the country.

There are plenty of local fresh
ingredients to pair with the local
catch for both the restaurant and
home cuisine but I especially
enjoy grilled local lobster in
the Summer as it has a wonderful
flavor and is hard to beat. Cooking
is one of my greatest passions
and I have tried to pass this on
to my daughters who often cook
with me in the kitchen. I also
like discovering local beaches,
cycling and driving my cars.

Chefs tip:

The lentils can be substituted for other pulses, starches or salads and the lobster can be eaten without the sauce, but I do recommend a glass of wine with this and a Côtes du Rhône rosé is an ideal pairing.

KENNEBUNKPORT LOBSTER
ON BRAISED LENTILS AND ROSE BUTTER SAUCE
BY JONATHAN CARTWRIGHT

serves 4

ingredients

1 cup	lentils du Puy
¼ cup	root vegetables, brunoise
½ lb	unsalted butter
1½ cups	chicken stock
2	Maine lobsters, 1½ lb each
1 cup	Côtes du Rhône rosé
1 tsp	shallots, diced
1	sprig of lemon thyme
6	cracked black peppercorns
salt, pepper, cayenne pepper	
½	lemon, juice
2 tbsp	extra virgin olive oil

to serve:

selection of micro greens or picked herbs

method

Soak the lentils in cold water for 3 hours, sweat the root vegetable brunoise in a tablespoon of the butter for 2 minutes over a medium heat without color. Add the drained lentils and cover with approximately 1 cup of chicken stock. Cook until tender, simmering for approximately 15 minutes.

Steam the lobsters for 5 minutes, cut in half, clean out the head area and cut open the claws and knuckles (this can be prepared up to a day beforehand).

Reduce the rosé wine with the shallots, thyme and peppercorns by half, add the remaining ½ cup of chicken stock and reduce by half again. Then slowly whisk in the remaining butter, season to taste with salt, pepper, cayenne and lemon juice. Strain and reserve in a warm spot until the dish is ready for saucing.

Brush the lobster halves with the extra virgin olive oil and grill for 3 minutes, flesh side down. Then turn the lobster over so the shell side is down on the grill bars for 3 minutes until cooked and hot.

to serve:

Place the lentils in the center of a plate and arrange the grilled lobster on top, sauce over and around the lobster, sprinkle micro greens or herbs on top and serve.

PAN ROASTED SCALLOPS,
SWEET CORN SUCCOTASH, FRIED OKRA
BY DALE MACKAY

The sweet and crunchy scallops combined with the creamy and savory corn really makes this dish a hit!

Dale Mackay

DALE MACKAY

I have a son, Ayden and I live in Vancouver, British Columbia, Canada. Originally I am from Saskatoon, Saskatchewan, Canada. This recipe makes for a great at-home dish because the ingredients are widely available, no matter where you live. I also liked including the okra, as not everyone knows how to use it. I've introduced it as the versatile fruit it is, hoping you'll give it a try.

My favorite ingredient? I love morels in the Springtime. They aren't just a mushroom: they're an event. I can go foraging for them about 2 hours away from the restaurant, which is a fantastic way to welcome the warm weather. They impart such an earthy yet delicate flavor. I particularly like to serve them with fish.

My favorite thing to do is spend time with my son. Beyond that, I enjoy Martial Arts. In fact, I just took a trip in March to compete in Thailand — it's such a great way to stay in shape and get an amazing adrenaline rush at the same time.

Chefs tip:

When preparing the corn purée whisk until the natural starches have thickened and the grainy texture of the starches has dissipated.

PAN ROASTED SCALLOPS,
SWEET CORN SUCCOTASH, FRIED OKRA

BY DALE MACKAY

serves 4

ingredients

scallops:

8	Qualicum Bay Scallops, muscle removed and sliced in half horizontally
3 tbsp	cornmeal
½ tsp	Madras curry
	salt & ground white pepper
	olive oil, as needed

corn purée:

4 cups	corn kernels
4 tbsp	milk

sweet corn succotash:

3	fresh corn on the cob
1 tbsp	olive oil
2 oz	double smoked bacon, small batons
1 tbsp	minced onion
1 tsp	minced red bird's eye chilis, seeded, finely diced and blanched 3 times
3	leaves of romaine heart, finely sliced
¼ cup	cream
¼ cup	corn purée (see above)
1 tsp	mascarpone cheese

tempura fried okra:

4 tbsp	tempura flour
½ tsp	Madras curry powder
	soda water, as needed
4	fresh okra
	vegetable oil, as needed

to serve:

4 oz	fresh purslane lettuce (substitute watercress leaves if not available)
	vegetable oil, as needed

Chef's tip:
Do not slice the okra in advance as it will weep moisture.

method

scallops:

Combine the cornmeal and Madras curry powder. Season the scallop slices with salt and pepper on both sides and coat the cut side of the scallops with cornmeal mixture, set aside.

corn purée:

Place the corn kernels in a blender and pulse until pasty. Add the milk and continue to purée until smooth. Strain through a fine meshed sieve into a heavy-bottomed saucepot. Cook over a medium-low heat, whisking constantly for approximately 15 minutes.

sweet corn succotash:

Trim the kernels from the corn stalk. Heat the oil in a large sauté pan over a medium heat and add the bacon. Cook, stirring, until the bacon becomes crispy. Add the onion and sauté until translucent, about 2 minutes. Add the chili and corn kernels and cook, stirring, until tender. Stir in the romaine lettuce, cream, and corn purée and simmer until reduced by half. Mix in the mascarpone cream, season to taste, and keep warm until ready to serve.

tempura fried okra:

In a small bowl, whisk the tempura flour and curry powder with enough soda water to yield a coating consistency. Fill a small saucepot one-third with vegetable oil and heat to 350°F. When ready to serve, slice the okra into ½" thick rounds and coat with tempura batter. Using a fork, transfer the okra to the oil, and fry until golden brown. Using a slotted spoon, transfer onto a paper towel-lined plate and sprinkle with salt.

to serve:

Heat a large sauté pan with enough oil to coat the bottom. Add the scallop slices cornmeal side-down in a single layer and sear until golden brown. Flip the scallops, cook for about 10 seconds on the other side and remove. Spoon the succotash into the middle of four heated appetizer plates. Arrange four pieces of scallop on top of each serving, scatter with fried okra, and garnish each plate with lettuce and purée.

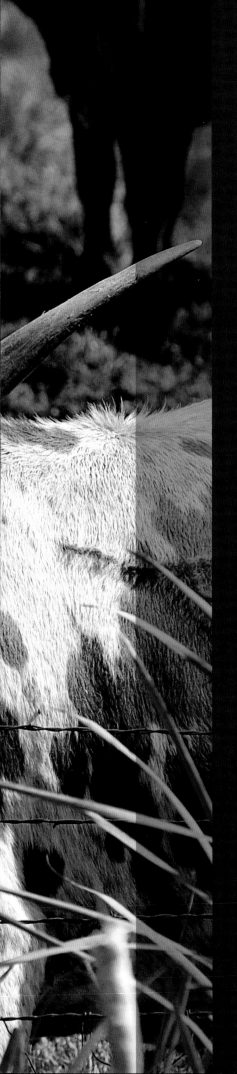

POULTRY, GAME & MEAT MAIN DISHES

For a meal to really bring people together there is nothing better than a rich and comforting meat dish. This selection of poultry, game and meat recipes has been lovingly chosen for you to try at home.

Grand Chef Christopher Brooks' 'Slow Roasted Pork' reminds him of childhood Sunday lunches with his famous 'Grandad Barry's Roast Potatoes'. Poultry favorites such as Grand Chef Daniel Humm's 'Organic Roast Chicken' and new takes on a classic with a 'Duck Burger' by Christophe Grosjean are all in this section

PAPPARDELLE
ALLA BOLOGNESE

BY AJ BLACK

*A classic bolognese sauce with a
sophisticated flair is Chef AJ Black's
trademark cuisine.*

AJ BLACK

I live with my wife Joelene and our two daughters Sophia and Stella, who divide their time between our home and restaurant in Edgartown on Martha's Vineyard, Massachusetts and Sanibel Island, Florida. Originally I am from the Messina area, in Sicily, Italy.

My favorite ingredient is fish and all types of seafood, and incidentally my favorite hobbies all relate to the sea too! As well as cooking, I enjoy boating and fishing. I have chosen this home dish because it's the perfect dish for family dinner parties and we have it regularly.

> "the perfect dish for family dinner parties"

PAPPARDELLE ALLA BOLOGNESE

BY AJ BLACK

serves 6

ingredients

bolognese:

1	small carrot
½	red onion
2	stalks of celery hearts
2	cloves of fresh garlic
good olive oil	
sea salt & white pepper	
1 tbsp	Italian basil, coarsely chopped
1 tsp	oregano, coarsely chopped
2-4	sage leaves, coarsely chopped
½ tsp	tarragon, coarsely chopped
1 tbsp	Italian parsley, coarsely chopped
½ lb	ground veal
½ lb	ground lamb
½ lb	ground pork
½ cup	good dry white Italian wine
½ cup	veal stock
2	8oz cans of San Marsano plum tomatoes
½	can of cherry tomatoes

to serve:

pasta of your choice	
6 oz	fresh heavy cream
18 oz	grated imported Parmigiano Reggiano cheese
½ cup	fresh Italian parsley, coarsely chopped

method

bolognese:

Purée the vegetables until super-fine in a food processor. In a medium stock pot, lightly coat the bottom with olive oil and lightly brown the vegetables, adding a pinch of sea salt and a dash of white pepper. Tie the fresh herbs together and add to the pot. Cook until the vegetables are browned and the liquid has evaporated.

Combine the ground meats and add to the vegetables until cooked through, adding more salt and pepper to taste. Follow by deglazing the cooked mixture with the dry white wine. This will lift up all the bits of flavor from the pan. Simmer until the wine is reduced.

Then add the veal stock and the cans of tomatoes, hand-crushing them while putting them in. The sauce should be smooth with small uniform pieces of meat. Aggressively stir in to get rid of any large chunks of meat or tomato. Bring to a quick boil on a high heat, then reduce to a simmer for about 30 minutes, stirring occasionally until the sauce is reduced to a quarter of its volume. Season to taste with salt and pepper. Leave the sauce to rest for at least 2 hours, skim off the excess fat and remove the herbs.

to serve:

Boil the pasta to three-quarters done. Add the meat sauce to a sauté pan with the heavy cream. Cook until the cream is reduced. Then add the pasta, and toss in 2 tablespoons of grated Parmigiano Reggiano cheese per serving and simmer until the pasta is al dente. Serve by lightly twisting into the dish, pour over any remaining sauce and top with more Parmigiano Reggiano and the parsley.

SEARED MUSCOVY DUCK BREAST,

GIZZARDS AND BEET

BY JEAN-FRANCOIS HEBERT

An easy to prepare, convenient dish great for any occasion.
Muscovy duck breast is a raised regional farm meat –
people really like to try local products.

ROLAND MENARD AND FRANCIS WOLF

As a duo we complement each other in the kitchen; with Roland's great cooking skills it is no wonder that we have won a great many awards for Manoir Hovey's restaurant. We both like to push for seasonal and local cuisine and use organic wherever possible.

Francis really injects fresh ideas into the kitchen and because of this we're well known for contemporary dishes that push the envelope in terms of textures and presentation. He is the one who introduced gadgets such as sous vide sealers and the Rolls-Royce of sorbet makers, the Pacojet.

ROLAND MENARD

I have three kids and two grand kids, I was born in Magog, Québec and currently live there. My hobbies include guitar, golf and teaching as well as cooking for my family and friends. My favorite ingredient is anything fresh, like fruit and vegetables from the market.

FRANCIS WOLF

I have two children — a full-time hobby in itself! I am glad to be able to live in Sherbrooke, my native town, a mere 20-minute drive from Manoir Hovey.

My favorite ingredients are the game meats of my native Québec especially venison from my own hunting expeditions.

This dish is by Sous Chef Jean-François Hébert, his motto is "everything done should be done well" and I agree. I cook this dish at home a lot, it's an easy-to-prepare, convenient dish which is great for any occasion.

"it's an easy to prepare, convenient dish which is great for any occasion"

SEARED MUSCOVY DUCK BREAST,
GIZZARDS AND BEET

BY JEAN-FRANCOIS HEBERT

serves 6

ingredients

duck:

3	duck breasts, preferably Muscovy

beet purée:

7 oz	yellow beet
1	French shallot, diced
1 tsp	turmeric
1 tsp	vinegar
1 tsp	paprika

thyme sauce:

2	French shallots, diced
3	branches of thyme or ¼ tsp dry thyme
½ cup	red wine
2 cups	chicken stock

garnish:

12	Brussels sprouts, cut in quarters and blanched in salted water
3	fresh kernels of corn
1	green shallot, thinly sliced
3 tbsp	butter
18	cured gizzards (optional). You can buy them already cured.
	salt & pepper

Chef's tip:

Evenly shaped slices make for a nicer presentation. Before searing the duck, trim the ends so that each breast is a perfect rectangle.

method

beet purée:

Cut the yellow beet into small cubes. Cook them in hot water for 15 minutes. Mix the cooked beetroot in a food processor to make a purée. Add the French shallot, turmeric, vinegar and paprika and purée until smooth.

seared muscovy duck breast and garnish:

Sear the duck in its fat at medium heat for 5-7 minutes. Then, flip the duck and finish cooking in the oven at 400°F for 7 minutes. Let the duck sit for 5 minutes before serving. Then slice each duck breast into six pieces. Meanwhile, cut the Brussels sprouts in to quarters and blanch them (cook them in boiling salted water for 3 minutes and cool them down in an ice bath). Sauté the vegetables (Brussels sprouts, corn and green shallot) in a pan with 3 tablespoons of butter and add the gizzards. Season with salt and pepper.

thyme sauce:

In a saucepan caramelize the French shallots and add the thyme. Add the red wine and reduce to a third, add the chicken stock and reduce to a third again.

to serve:

Spread the purée on the plate. Set the garnish over the purée, in the center of the plate. Place three gizzards over the purée then top this with three pieces of duck breast per plate. Pour the sauce over the duck breast and garnish.

AUBERGE SAINT-ANTOINE
QUEBEC CITY, QUEBEC, CANADA

VENISON RIBS
BBQ STYLE
WITH WINTER VEGETABLES

BY FRANCOIS BLAIS

*Here is a recipe that suits our restaurant
Panache's style; a simple recipe that
uses quality products found locally, and
prepared without pretension!*

> ## "venison is part of our culinary culture "

FRANCOIS BLAIS

I was born in Québec City and I still live here. I have never worked outside of Québec province, only with great local chefs. I was named Best Québec Apprentice in 1999 and Chef of the Year (in Québec) in 2009! One of my favorite ingredients is maple syrup (are you surprised?), it's so good with almost anything! I have chosen venison BBQ ribs because it's such a great feeling eating them after a long day outside in Winter time. Venison is also part of our culinary culture.

After work and taking care of my family, one of my favorite activities is biking. It's a great way to stay healthy and it's good for the body as well as the mind. It's also a great way of traveling — you see so many more things on a bike than you can when you sit in a car! Imagine yourself on a bike in wine country!

VENISON RIBS BBQ STYLE
WITH WINTER VEGETABLES

BY FRANCOIS BLAIS

serves 4

ingredients

ribs:

3 tbsp	butter
4 lb	trimmed venison short ribs, cut into 4 equal pieces

BBQ sauce:

4	shallots, finely chopped
8	garlic cloves, finely chopped
1 tbsp	fresh ginger, finely chopped
½ cup	brown sugar
¼ cup	seasoned rice vinegar
½ tsp each	mustard grain, coriander, cardamom, anise seeds, dill seeds, bay leaves
½ cup	tomato paste
2 cups	venison stock or any brown stock available (such as veal stock)
1	lemon, zest and juice
salt & pepper	

vegetables 'papillotte':

any good	Winter vegetables such as carrots, turnips, baby beet, fingerling potatoes
1 tbsp	butter
1	shallot, thinly sliced
1	garlic clove, finely chopped
salt & pepper	

method

BBQ sauce:

Sweat the shallots, garlic and ginger in a medium-size saucepan, add the brown sugar, the vinegar and all the spices. When the brown sugar is completely dissolved, add all the remaining ingredients and simmer for about 30 minutes, then strain.

ribs:

Lightly brown the ribs in butter, add the BBQ sauce and simmer until done. Remove the ribs and reduce the sauce by a third. Glaze the ribs with enough sauce to keep the meat moist in a very hot oven or on the BBQ grill.

vegetables 'papillotte':

Carefully clean and peel all the vegetables. Put them in a big piece of aluminium foil with the butter, shallot and garlic. Season with salt and pepper and close the foil. Put in a hot oven until the vegetables are done. It should take about 1 hour depending on the size of the vegetables.

to serve:

Serve the glazed venison ribs with the vegetables and a little more sauce.

SLOW ROASTED PORK
AND GRANDAD BARRY'S ROAST POTATOES SERVED WITH SAVOY CABBAGE
BY CHRISTOPHER BROOKS

My Dad, Barry Brooks, made these potatoes for years at our home in England. The secret is the pan juices and fat from the roasting meat and the high heat. They are still a favorite when I go home and they have now become a staple for my family and friends in Lenox, Massachusetts. My children call them Grandad Barry's Potatoes.

CHRISTOPHER BROOKS

I'm from London, England, but now live here and my wife is American. I have one child and two stepchildren and I don't live far from Blantyre in Lenox Dale. In fact I actually walk to work in the Summer months. The pork recipe that I have chosen as my at-home dish is quite close to my heart as my Dad cooked this dish 'forever' for Sunday lunch — it's very much a family tradition.

I love using celeriac (celery root) as it is so versatile — it can be puréed, steamed, fried, roasted, braised, glazed and used raw. Plus it can be paired with other ingredients for appetizers, entrées, used with fish, with meat, in salads and even in desserts! To relax I enjoy a round of golf, I'm quite interested in cars, and of course, soccer.

Chef's tip:
Apple sauce is a good side dish and grain mustard is a nice touch. Crispy bacon into the cabbage adds another dimension.

SLOW ROASTED PORK
AND GRANDAD BARRY'S ROAST POTATOES
SERVED WITH SAVOY CABBAGE

BY CHRISTOPHER BROOKS

serves 6

ingredients

roast pork:

5-6 lb	boneless pork butt (rump cut)
salt & pepper	
vegetable oil for browning meat	
4	sprigs of fresh thyme
2	red apples (a hard variety), unpeeled and diced

potatoes:

russet potatoes – enough to have 6 servings
salted water
½ cup   reserved pan juices and fat from roasting meat (or more)
salt & pepper

cabbage:

3 lb   head of Savoy cabbage
salted water
2 tbsp   butter
black pepper
crispy bacon (optional)
1 tbsp   fresh parsley, chopped

method

roast pork:

Preheat a convection oven to 275°F/traditional oven 300°F. Season the meat with salt and pepper. Sear the meat on all sides in hot vegetable oil. Place in a roasting pan with the thyme and diced apples (the herbs and apples should be placed on top of the meat and not just in the pan). Roast, uncovered, for 4 hours. Every half an hour, baste with the pan juices. Start preparing the potatoes (see below). Remove from the oven, spoon out the fat and juices and reserve. Turn the heat up to 400°F convection/450°F traditional oven and return the meat to the oven, still uncovered, for 1 hour. Baste once or twice. Now put the potatoes in the oven in their own pan, seasoned with half a cup or more of the meat juices. After 1 hour, remove the meat and let rest for 30 minutes, uncovered, before carving (the potatoes remain in the oven until done).

potatoes:

For the potatoes, peel and cut into large uniform chunks. Bring to a boil in salted water and cook until almost done. Place into their own roasting pan. Use half a cup of the reserved meat pan juices and fat to coat the potatoes and season lightly. Do not cover the pan. Put into the oven with the meat. Roast for 1 hour and 15 minutes (turning once) or until golden, crunchy brown and still fluffy inside.

cabbage:

For the cabbage, remove the thickest part of the spine. Shred into ½" strips, blanch in boiling salted water until tender (this will not take long). Strain and place in a serving bowl with butter and black pepper to taste (crispy bacon can be added if desired). Sprinkle with the parsley.

to serve:

Carve the pork, and serve with the potatoes and cabbage – pan juices may also be served.

ROASTED ORGANIC CHICKEN
WITH LEMON AND ROSEMARY

BY DANIEL HUMM

An easy way to turn the classic roasted chicken into a decadent feast.

DANIEL HUMM

I am from Zurich, Switzerland and live in New York with my wife. I have two daughters – Justine, and Vivienne. I have lived in the United States since 2003 when I became Executive Chef of Campton Place in San Francisco. I moved three years later to Eleven Madison Park and have been there since. We have recently received Grand Chef status and I enjoy being part of the Relais and Châteaux family.

I have chosen this roasted chicken dish because it brings comfort and luxury in the same recipe. I love the different seasons and all the treasures they bring with them, it means you can discover the same ingredients again and again. My hobbies include running and biking – I like to keep fit.

"comfort and luxury in the same recipe"

ROASTED ORGANIC CHICKEN
WITH LEMON AND ROSEMARY

BY DANIEL HUMM

serves 4

ingredients

stuffing:

1¾ cups	butter, softened
1 cup	brioche breadcrumbs
2 tbsp	rosemary, minced
2 tsp	lemon, zest
salt & pepper	

chicken:

1	whole organic chicken, 4lb approximately
5	sprigs of rosemary
2	garlic cloves, peeled
1	lemon, whole

method

stuffing:

Preheat the oven to 380°F.

Combine the butter with the breadcrumbs, rosemary and lemon zest. Season to taste with salt and pepper. Place the stuffing into a piping bag.

chicken:

Run your finger under the skin, separating the skin from the meat (from the head side of the bird), being careful to leave it attached at the center of the sternum, so as to help keep the shape of the two breasts during roasting. Be careful to not tear the skin. Pipe the brioche stuffing under the skin of the legs and breasts. Ensure that there is an even distribution and that a good shape is maintained. Season the inside of the bird with salt. Fill the cavity with the sprigs of rosemary, garlic cloves and the whole lemon that has been pricked with a knife to release the aroma. Truss the bird by hand with twine. Chill in a refrigerator to set the butter and shape. Roast in the oven for about 45 minutes, rotating the bird after 20 minutes. (Cooking time will vary with the size of the bird.)

to serve:

Let the chicken rest for 15 minutes before carving.

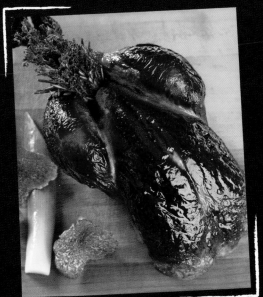

FOUR STORY HILL
FARM POULARDE

BY THOMAS KELLER

prefer one-pot meals – chicken is great for that'

THOMAS KELLER

I spend most of my time in Yountville, a small town in California's Napa Valley. I was born in Oceanside, California and raised in Florida.

Whenever I cook at home, I like things to be easy so I prefer one-pot meals — chicken is great for that. My favorite ingredient? Salt. It can be used for everything and is very versatile. The key is to utilize it in a controlled way. For relaxation I enjoy golfing. It's great to get out on the course and focus on improving my game.

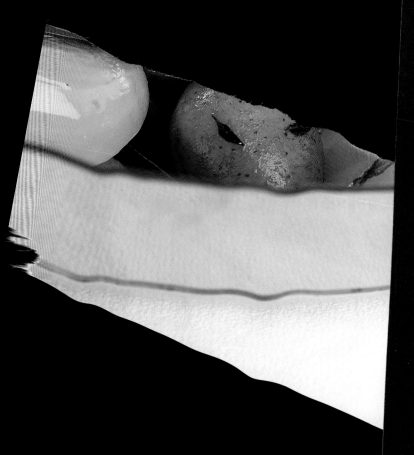

" I like things to be easy so I

FOUR STORY HILL FARM POULARDE

BY THOMAS KELLER

serves 4

ingredients

1	poularde, 4-5 lb
	salt & pepper, to taste
2 tbsp	butter
½	bunch of thyme
3	cloves garlic, crushed
	olive oil
	root vegetables (spring garlic, Tokyo turnips, marble potatoes, etc) as desired

method

Submerge the poularde in a 5% salt/water solution for 30 minutes. Allow to dry on a plate, uncovered, for 12 hours in a refrigerator.

Preheat the oven to 350°F. Season the poularde liberally with salt and pepper, and brush with butter. Stuff the cavity with thyme and garlic then truss the bird with butcher's twine. Place the poularde on top of a bed of clean, trimmed root vegetables cut to uniform size. Add olive oil to coat the vegetables as required. Roast in the oven, basting often with the fat from the pan, until the poularde is just cooked through and the juices run clear. Allow to rest for at least 10 minutes before carving.

to serve:

Carve the bird into eight pieces so that each guest enjoys both the white and dark meat. Serve over a bed of the roast vegetables.

Chef's tip:

A poularde is a young male chicken that has been spayed, making it extra plump. If no source of poularde is available a regular chicken of the same size can be substituted.

This is a great simple dish. Roasting root vegetables brings
out their natural sweetness, which couples beautifully with
the herbs and the beef. Quick and easy but amazing at the
same time, this dish also works well with chicken.

ROASTED CHATEAUBRIAND
WITH CARAMELIZED ROOT VEGETABLES
BY JOE SCHAFER

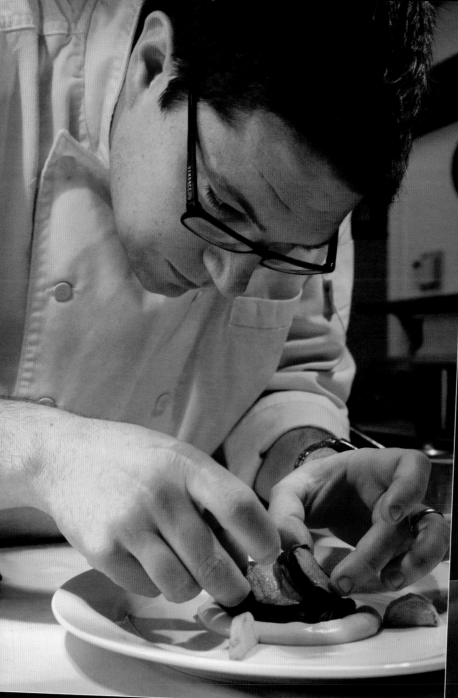

JOE SCHAFER

I received an Associates Degree from New England Culinary Institute in Essex Junction, Vermont. I have worked at several Relais & Châteaux properties including Lake Placid Lodge, Triple Creek Ranch, Restaurant Hélène Darroze and The White Barn Inn. My food is heavily influenced by classic French technique focusing on seasonal ingredients and local products. We strive to make food fitting to Glendorn's surroundings of rustic elegance and comfortable sophistication.

I am originally from upstate New York and my wife is from coastal Maine. We reside in Bradford, PA with our young son. We enjoy the quiet life of a small town. When I cook at home I always keep two things in mind. Simplicity and an easy clean up. I am a big fan of one-pot dinners. After a long day at work or a day off I want something simple, honest and quick.

"after a long day at work or a day off I want something simple, honest and quick"

ROASTED CHATEAUBRIAND
WITH CARAMELIZED ROOT VEGETABLES

BY JOE SCHAFER

serves 4

ingredients

1	center cut beef tenderloin
olive oil	
chopped herbs	
2	parsnips
1	bunch of baby carrots
10	fingerling potatoes
1	sprig of thyme
1	sprig of rosemary
salt & pepper	
2	heads of garlic
red wine	
butter	

method

Rub the beef with olive oil and chopped thyme and rosemary until covered. Clean, peel and wash the vegetables. Toss with olive oil and whole herbs. Season with salt and pepper. Cut the heads of the garlic in half. Place the beef in the center of a pan, and arrange the vegetables, garlic and potatoes around the meat. Place in a 350°F oven and cook until it reaches an internal temperature of 135°F. Let rest for 10 minutes. Remove any pan juices, and add red wine and a few tabs of butter for a light gravy.

to serve:

Carve into slices and serve with the vegetables.

Chefs tip:
Try adding Brussels sprouts to give an added dimension to the dish.

143

This is my favorite grilling meal for the Summer. We grill outside for dinner almost exclusively (fewer pots and pans to clean up.) We live in the heart of grass-fed beef country and in our lush Alpine Valley the cattle grow quickly and healthy. So we feel good about eating beef here, especially when it is raised on our sister ranch.

GRILLED BEEF TENDERLOIN,
MARINATED GRILLED VEGETABLES WITH SMOKY TOMATO VINAIGRETTE

BY CLYDE NELSON

CLYDE NELSON

I moved into my home on Home Ranch 20 years ago, as Head Chef, accompanied by my wife and two sons and I've never wanted to leave. It's the perfect life, a great job and the ideal environment for bringing up a family. In my spare time, I referee soccer games — I coached my boys when they were young and it just grew from there — and I ski. Cross-country skiing is a passion of mine. I ski to work in the Winter but my favorite time is right at the end of the season when most people have gone home and I have the slopes to myself.

The vegetables from my garden and the eggs from my neighbors' chickens are my favorite ingredients, then of course there's an abundance of great beef around here. The dish I have recreated is one that we eat regularly as a family — we cook outdoors most days in the Summer and this is a real favorite — and it includes my home-grown vegetables.

Chef's tip:

Arrange a thicker layer of coals at one end of the barbecue for a hotter fire. Place the grill about 6" above the heat. Use an instant-read thermometer to check the internal meat temperature. Reserve any remaining marinade to use as dipping oil for hot crusty French bread.

GRILLED BEEF TENDERLOIN,
MARINATED GRILLED VEGETABLES WITH SMOKY TOMATO VINAIGRETTE

BY CLYDE NELSON

serves 10-12

ingredients

1	whole beef tenderloin, 4-5 lb

dry rub:

3 tbsp	kosher salt
3 tbsp	coarsely ground black pepper
2 tbsp	garlic, minced
1 tbsp	paprika
2 tsp	bay leaf, minced
1½ tsp	cayenne pepper
1½ tsp	dry mustard
¼ cup	fresh parsley, chopped
1 tbsp	sugar

barbecue mop:

1 cup	beef broth
¼ cup	red wine
¼ cup	Worcestershire sauce
2 tbsp	canola oil
2	Serrano or jalapeno chilies, crushed
3 tbsp	bottled barbecue sauce

marinade:

1 cup	olive oil
¼ cup	fresh basil leaves
3-4	sprigs of fresh parsley
1	shallot, peeled
1	large garlic clove, peeled
2	leaves of fresh sage
1 tbsp	lemon juice
1½ tsp	parmesan cheese, grated
1½ tsp	pine nuts

vegetables:

2	Japanese eggplants
2	red bell peppers
1	small jicama
1	bunch of scallions
8	stalks of asparagus, trimmed

smoky tomato vinaigrette:

2-4	Roma tomatoes
2 tbsp	each of fresh basil, fresh marjoram, fresh tarragon, fresh thyme, fresh fennel, all chopped
2 tbsp	lemon juice or wine vinegar
1 large	shallot, peeled, coarsely chopped
½ cup	extra virgin olive oil

method

dry rub:

Oil your hands with 3 tablespoons of vegetable oil and rub over the beef. Combine the dry rub ingredients and rub over the beef. Allow to sit for 20-30 minutes. Meanwhile, prepare the charcoal for grilling.

barbecue mop:

Combine the ingredients and season with salt and pepper. Place the tenderloin over white-hot coals and sear on one side for 5 minutes. Brush with the mopping sauce, turn the roast 90 degrees to make criss-cross grill marks and grill for another 5 minutes. Turn the roast over and grill for another 5 minutes, continuing to mop every 5 minutes. Turn two more times to sear all sides. When it reaches 120°F internally move the meat to the coolest part of the grill and cover loosely with aluminium foil. Rest for 10-15 minutes. The temperature should then be 124°F to 130°F. For medium-rare cook until 135°F.

marinade:

Combine all the ingredients in a food processor or blender. Season with salt and pepper and purée.

vegetables:

Halve the eggplants lengthwise. Remove the seeds from the peppers and cut into thirds. Peel the jicama and slice ¼" thick. Place all the vegetables in a shallow baking pan and drizzle with enough marinade to coat lightly. Marinate at room temperature for 1 hour. Grill for 10-15 minutes, turning occasionally and basting with the marinade until lightly browned and tender.

smoky tomato vinaigrette:

Grill or smoke the tomatoes until the skin begins to cook. Peel off the skin, cut crosswise, and squeeze out the seeds. Dice and place in a sieve to drain for a few minutes. Combine with the herbs in a bowl. Add the lemon juice and shallot, and gradually whisk in the olive oil.

to serve:

Slice the beef and serve with the vegetables and vinaigrette.

THOMAS HENKELMANN — HOMESTEAD INN
GREENWICH, CONNECTICUT, USA

MACARONI AND CHEESE
WITH SEARED FOIE GRAS
BY THOMAS HENKELMANN

Home and hearth with a little slice of decadence and rich round flavors that coddle the soul.

THOMAS HENKELMANN

I have always tried to produce my interpretation of French food. It is my passion and my life and together with classic French training and my German background I have been inspired by all.

I was born in the Black Forest in Germany but moved to Paris to learn French. I moved to New York in 1989 and set up my restaurant, Thomas Henkelmann, in 1997.

I have three children who are all grown up now: two daughters, one in Baltimore, Maryland and one in Greenwich, Connecticut and a son who lives in Colorado Springs, Colorado.

In my spare time I like to play tennis, take part in downhill skiing and I also enjoy platform tennis which is great to play even when it's cold.

I have chosen the macaroni and cheese as my at-home recipe because it personifies comfort and family for most people. I serve it with foie gras in the restaurant, but at home I garnish the macaroni and cheese with a dollop of tomato fondue. Although I am reticent to name a favorite ingredient I do believe that rich flavorful stocks are essential for cooking in all seasons.

ThH

" it personifies comfort and family for most people "

MACARONI AND CHEESE
WITH SEARED FOIE GRAS

BY THOMAS HENKELMANN

serves 6

ingredients

cheese sauce:

½ oz	unsalted butter
1	shallot, finely diced
¼	garlic clove, finely diced
3 oz	chicken stock
3 oz	heavy cream
½	bay leaf
½ lb	mild Cheddar cheese, grated

salt, fresh white pepper & cayenne

apples:

1	Granny Smith apple, peeled, cored and cut into 12 equally-sized wedges
4 oz	water
1 oz	dry white wine
1	lemon, juice
2 oz	granulated sugar
1 oz	confectioner's sugar

to serve:

6 oz	cavatappi pasta (or pasta of choice), cooked in salt water until al dente
6 oz	Hudson Valley duck foie gras, sliced and seasoned with salt and freshly ground pepper
6	cheese sticks
6	twigs of chervil

method

cheese sauce:

In a sautéuse melt the butter, add the shallot and garlic. Sweat until tender, then add the chicken stock, heavy cream and ½ bay leaf. Bring to a boil and simmer on a low heat for approximately 8 minutes. Strain the sauce and then add the cheese and season to taste, whisking until smooth. Keep warm until needed (do not boil the sauce once the cheese has been added).

apples:

Bring the water, dry white wine, lemon juice and granulated sugar to a boil. Add the apple wedges and simmer until tender. When needed remove from the liquid, dry the wedges and set in a non-stick frying pan that has been powdered with the confectioner's sugar. Heat the pan to caramelize the sugar. Once the apple wedges have their desired color, turn the apples over and keep warm.

to serve:

Rinse the pasta under hot water, until warm. Drain and add to the warm cheese sauce, reheat the sauce while stirring. Portion into six warm soup plates, set two apple wedges on top of each serving. Sauté the foie gras, set on top of the apple wedges, garnish with a cheese stick and some chervil.

Chefs tip:
You may substitute the foie gras with sautéed shrimps and a little bit of tomato fondue if you wish.

THE INN OF THE FIVE GRACES

SANTE FE, NEW MEXICO, USA

CHICKEN MOLE,
GARLIC MASHED POTATOES
AND CALABACITAS

BY MICHAEL ROYBAL

*A personal favorite, this is the ultimate
Mexican dish. The chocolate works really
well with the meat!*

MICHAEL ROYBAL

I was born and raised in 'the land of enchantment', Santa Fe, New Mexico, a few doors away from the now famous Pink Adobe. I had a big family growing up, six brothers and three sisters, and Santa Fe is where my wife and our families have been for many generations. It is a beautiful high desert with colorful skies, many cultures and lots of chili!

My favorite ingredients are red and green chilis and I like working closely with local farmers, ensuring the freshest ingredients. My hobbies are fishing, camping, weight training, softball, basketball and playing the guitar.

Chefs tip:

The mashed potatoes may be made a day ahead and reheated before serving. The mole sauce ingredients must be roasted separately because some ingredients roast faster than others.

CHICKEN MOLE,
GARLIC MASHED POTATOES AND CALABACITAS

BY MICHAEL ROYBAL

serves 4

ingredients

chicken:

4	boneless, skin on chicken breasts, 7 oz each
¼ cup	vegetable oil, for frying
1 tsp	red chili powder
½ tsp	smoked paprika
½ tsp	garlic powder
½ tsp	salt

mole sauce:

2 oz	dried ancho (pablano) chili pods, seeds and stems removed
3 cups	chicken broth
1 tbsp	sesame seeds
2 oz	pepitas (shelled pumpkin seeds)
1 oz	almonds
1 oz	French bread, cut into small cubes
¼ cup	crushed animal crackers
½	banana
2 tbsp	golden raisins
1	clove garlic
½ oz	Mexican chocolate
¼ tsp	ground cumin
salt, to taste	

garlic mashed potatoes:

3	boiled potatoes, cut up
2	cloves garlic, peeled and diced
¼ cup	butter
½ cup	half and half
salt, to taste	

calabacitas:

2 tbsp	onion, diced
1 tbsp	butter
1	clove garlic, minced
¼ cup	whole kernel sweet corn
1 cup	zucchini, medium diced
1 cup	yellow squash, medium diced

garnish:

1	blue corn tortilla (optional)
1 tbsp	oil, for frying
2 tbsp	Cheddar cheese, grated

method

chicken:

Preheat the oven to 350°F. Generously sprinkle and rub the chicken breasts with the spices and salt. Sear skin side down with oil in a skillet over a medium heat until lightly browned, about 3-5 minutes. Turn the chicken breasts over and place in the oven to finish cooking, about 5-10 minutes.

mole sauce:

In a medium saucepan, simmer the chili pods in the broth for 20 minutes. Meanwhile, in a fry pan over a medium heat, lightly roast the sesame seeds, pepitas, almonds, bread, crackers, banana, raisins and garlic each separately and reserve. Add the roasted ingredients and chocolate to the simmered chili pods and broth and purée in a blender. Return to the saucepan, stir in the cumin and salt.

garlic mashed potatoes:

In a medium pan over a low heat, lightly sauté the garlic in 1 tablespoon of butter until opaque. Add the potatoes, half and half and the remaining butter and heat on low, stirring frequently until hot. Season.

calabacitas:

In a skillet over a medium heat, sauté the onions in butter until opaque, add the garlic and cook until fragrant, about 30 seconds. Add the corn, zucchini and squash and cook until heated through but still crunchy.

tortilla strips:

Cut the tortilla into thin strips, lightly fry in oil in a fry pan over a medium heat until just crisp, remove from the heat, drain and reserve.

to serve:

Place the potatoes and calabacitas on warm plates, add a chicken breast, and sprinkle with Cheddar, ladle over the sauce and garnish with tortilla strips, if using.

155

"I like working closely with local farmers, ensuring the freshest ingredients"

POTATOES THAT TASTE BETTER THAN THE CHICKEN

BY JEAN-GEORGES VONGERICHTEN

Every once in a while, we'll have unexpected guests drop by our country home on the weekends. Of course, I want to be able to welcome them with a feast and, with such short notice, this is my go-to dish. It's as simple as can be – Roasted Chicken with Golden Potatoes – but it's the most flavorsome chicken and potatoes you will ever eat. I like to say that the potatoes taste better than the chicken, because they've been soaking up the juices at the bottom of the roasting pan, and have turned the perfect golden brown. It's always a crowd pleaser!

159

JEAN-GEORGES VONGERICHTEN

I have three children, Cedric, Louise, and Chloe. All of them live in New York City although Louise and Cedric were born and raised mostly in France.

Chloe, the youngest of the three, was born and raised in New York.

I chose this dish because it is my go-to dish when unexpected guests show up for dinner. Even though it takes some time to roast, the prep is quick and the result is an incredibly flavorful dish. It's always a hit with my friends!

Chilies are my favorite ingredient. Thai chilies, jalapenos, serranos, anything that gives a dish a good kick is in my pantry — I have trouble keeping peppers out of my dishes!

I have recently started keeping bees and I have been consumed by the hobby, though it's a Summer pastime only. In the Winter, I like to ice skate and ski whenever I get the chance.

"my go-to dish when unexpected guests show up for dinner"

POTATOES THAT TASTE BETTER THAN THE CHICKEN

BY JEAN-GEORGES VONGERICHTEN

serves 4

ingredients

2 lb	Yukon Gold potatoes
6 tbsp	butter
½ cup	grapeseed oil
1	chicken 2½-3lb, with liver
salt & pepper	
rosemary branch	
thyme branch	
2 tbsp	water
fleur de sel	

method

Peel and cut the potatoes into large dice about 1″ thick. Butter a roasting pan with half the butter and half the oil. Put a single layer of potatoes in the pan.

Season the chicken inside and out with salt and pepper. Stuff the rosemary and thyme into the cavity with the liver. Push the bird leg side down into the potatoes. Rub the remaining oil and butter over the top side of the skin.

Put in a 450°F oven for 18 minutes. Flip the chicken on to its other leg and cook for another 18 minutes. Then put the chicken breast side up, add the water and cook for 10 more minutes.

to serve:

Present the whole pan on the dining table and carve the chicken in the pan so its juices go into the potatoes. Serve the chicken and spoon the jus over it. Serve potatoes with a little fleur de sel sprinkled on top.

DUCK BURGER
BY CHRISTOPHE GROSJEAN

The most well known American signature dish all over the world, approached by a French guy who grew up in Burgundy and took it to the next level.

CHRISTOPHE GROSJEAN

My love of food started when I was very young and was influenced by my grandmother who taught me to love the land, embrace great food and love your family. I'm from France and worked throughout the region before I moved to the Monterey Peninsula. I especially enjoy cooking with fresh ingredients and utilize them when they are in season. I really look for new ways to cook things so that they look as natural and fresh as possible.

When I have time I like to garden; I grow all the herbs I use at the restaurant. I also try to ride my mountain bike or road bike as much as possible. I love being out in the middle of the forest; it's a good feeling. Very different from spending 12 hours in the kitchen. And of course, my main free time is spent with my children and my beautiful, supportive wife. I truly believe the success of a chef is due to his wife! It's important to have a strong support system at home to keep one calm.

"I especially enjoy cooking with fresh ingredients and utilize them when they are in season"

DUCK BURGER

BY CHRISTOPHE GROSJEAN

serves 6

ingredients

4	duck breasts
6	large slices of foie gras

to serve:

6	burger buns
2 oz	blackcurrant mustard
6	butter lettuce leaves

chips or duck fat fries, to serve

method

Separate the skin from the breast of the duck, keep one piece of skin for later. Place the skin and the breasts in the freezer for a couple of minutes, as this helps the meat to keep its texture. Grind the mix, and form into six patties. Reserve in the fridge.

Cook the patties until medium, sear the foie gras in a non-stick cast iron pan, medium as well.

to serve:

Toast the burger bun and add some blackcurrant mustard. Place a lettuce leaf on the bottom bun, top with the patty, followed by the foie gras and finish with the top bun. Serve immediately with chips or duck fat fries.

Chef's tip:
The ratio of meat and fat should be 80/20 for the duck patty.

BRAISED
VEAL CHEEK
AND PARSNIP PUREE
WITH BOURBON VANILLA
BY JEAN-FRANCOIS BELAIR

*Braised veal cheek is a hearty dish and
an ideal recipe for the colder months.
Root vegetables hark back to the time of
underground caverns and the long Winter
months endured by our ancestors.*

JEAN-FRANCOIS BELAIR

I'm from Montréal and I live in La Malbaie. I began cooking when I was 16 and had my first job in a restaurant in Longueuil. I have worked for a few Relais & Châteaux properties and have briefly worked in France. On my days off I like to go fishing and mushroom picking. My favorite foods are fish soup and shellfish but my favorite ingredients are all the fruits and vegetables from Québec in Fall season, otherwise I love lemons!

I have chosen this recipe because braised veal cheek is a hearty dish and an ideal recipe for the colder months. Root vegetables hark back to the time of underground caverns and the long Winter months endured by our ancestors. I look at raw products to get inspiration and like to use traditional local ingredients.

"I look at raw products to get inspiration and like to use traditional local ingredients"

BRAISED VEAL CHEEK
AND PARSNIP PUREE WITH BOURBON VANILLA

BY JEAN-FRANCOIS BELAIR

serves 5

ingredients

veal cheeks:

2 lb 3 oz	suckling veal cheeks
	butter
2 lb 3 oz	mirepoix (a medley of diced onion, carrot and celery)
8½ pt	veal stock
1 pt	red wine
	star anise, to taste
	thyme, to taste
	rosemary, to taste
	laurel, to taste
	salt & pepper

parsnip purée:

2 lb 3 oz	parsnips, peeled and cut into large chunks
2 pt	milk
1	bourbon vanilla pod

method

veal cheeks:

Preheat the oven to 300°F. Trim the veal cheeks and season generously. Sear them in butter in a pot large enough to contain the meat, mirepoix, stock and wine. Put the lightly seared veal on the side and toss the mirepoix until it starts to brown. Deglaze with red wine and reduce for several minutes. Add the veal back with the mirepoix, star anise and herbs, and cover with the veal stock. Cook uncovered in the oven for at least 3 hours. When cooked and very tender, gently remove the cheeks, filter the cooking juice, return it to the pan and reduce to half. Season to taste.

parsnip purée:

Bring the parsnips to a boil in the milk and cook for 20 minutes. Remove the parsnips and purée them in a food processor. Split the vanilla pod in half lengthwise and scrape the interior using the tip of a knife to remove as many seeds as possible. Add the vanilla seeds to the purée while mixing in the food processor. Adjust the seasoning and garnish.

to serve:

Serve with seasonal vegetables.

ROAST PORK TENDERLOIN
WITH WINTER VEGETABLES, THYME AND APPLE
BY BRIAN SUTTON

Roasted and full of flavor, this dish is just what you need on a cold Winter's evening.

BRIAN SUTTON

I started my career as a part-time dishwasher in a pub in my hometown of Colchester, Essex in England. It was a nice pub, a gastro-pub in today's terms and it was the environment of working in the kitchens that made me want to become a chef. I studied at the Colchester Institute of Culinary Arts and put in an extra year in the pastry department to round out my expertise. I was then recruited to work in Charlottesville, Virginia with Executive Chef Mark Salter of The Inn at Perry Cabin. I did move back to Europe for a while to work in Cannes and then Switzerland, but then I returned to work in the U.S. under Daniel Boulud at Wynn Las Vegas.

At present I live in Saranac Lake New York although I do love to travel. The dish I have chosen is a great interpretation of the old English roast dinner and my favorite ingredient is olive oil. In my spare time, like all Englishmen, I love soccer.

"a great interpretation of the old English roast dinner"

ROAST PORK TENDERLOIN
WITH WINTER VEGETABLES, THYME AND APPLE

BY BRIAN SUTTON

serves 4

ingredients

2	pork tenderloins
½ cup	parsnips
½ cup	Brussels sprouts
½ cup	fingerling potatoes
1 qt	chicken stock
10	sprigs of thyme
salt & pepper	
2	Granny Smith apples
1	large sweet onion
extra virgin olive oil	

method

Peel the parsnips and cut into ½″ dice. Take the outer leaves off the Brussels sprouts and cut in half. Cut the potatoes to approximately the same size as the parsnips. Sauté the potatoes and parsnips in the oil, over a medium-high heat until golden brown, then add the Brussels sprouts and continue to cook for another 5-7 minutes. Reduce the chicken stock by half and add 5 sprigs of thyme about 10 minutes before serving, and adjust the seasoning.

Dice the apples and onions into ½″ dice and lay in an ovenproof dish with the remaining sprigs of thyme. Season the pork tenderloin with salt and pepper, and sear in the olive oil over a medium-high heat. Place the tenderloin on top of the apple/onion mixture and bake at 350°F until desired.

to serve:

Slice the pork tenderloin and serve with the roasted vegetables.

ELK AND CHOCOLATE CHILI

BY JONATHAN GUSHUE

I love this mixture of the gamey elk, sweet-hot chili and bitter chocolate. It really sets the tone for a warm ultra comforting meal. Definitely one of our Fall signature dishes.

JONATHAN GUSHUE

I was born and grew up in St. John's Newfoundland Canada and, after finishing school, I attended Georgian College for both Culinary Management and Hotel Management. I've worked in various places over the years including Japan, England and Canada. I have a wife, Karen and three children Tim, Nick and Allie and I love cooking together with them. I also like collecting cookbooks, running and playing ice hockey. From a cooking point of view I am especially interested in the Slow Food Canada movement and being able to spend time with farmers and producers.

So many farmers produce heirloom vegetables and outstanding ingredients in our area. My favorite ingredient is lobster from the grand banks of Newfoundland as it so sweet due to the cold waters. I also like elk in the Fall, especially when it is mixed with sweet-hot chili and bitter chocolate and, of course, citrus is the ultimate in refreshment. I can't imagine a better way to end a great meal!

ELK AND CHOCOLATE CHILI

BY JONATHAN GUSHUE

serves 6

ingredients

2 lb	elk sirloin, diced
2	cloves garlic, minced
1	red onion, diced
1 tbsp	sweet smoked paprika
1 tsp	chili powder
2 tbsp	tomato paste
3	Roma tomatoes chopped
3 tbsp	ground cumin
1 tbsp	red wine vinegar
2 cups	red wine
4 pt	veal stock

to serve:

4 oz	dark chocolate
	salt & black pepper
10 fl oz	Chèvre Blanc
7 oz	Chèvre Noir, 3 years old, grated
	scallions, chopped

method

Heat a large saucepan over a high heat. Brown the elk with the garlic and onion. Drain and clean out your pan. Add the paprika, chili, tomato paste, tomatoes, cumin, vinegar, and red wine. Reduce by half and add the seared elk and veal stock. Simmer for 45 minutes until the flavors meld.

to serve:

Fold in the chocolate and check for seasoning. Top with Chèvre Blanc, grated Chèvre Noir and scallions.

HAM EN CROUTE 'PAPA JO'
AND FINGERLING POTATO SALAD
BY JEAN JOHO

This recipe always makes me remember my home country. A potato salad always has to be made the same day and eaten at room temperature. This is a perfect Summer dish to enjoy on your patio at night or on a picnic. Serve with a glass of Alsace Pinot Blanc.

JEAN JOHO

I was born and raised in Alsace, France, and entered the profession at the young age of six, peeling vegetables and potatoes in my aunt's restaurant kitchen. That humble beginning ignited a lifetime of studying, discovering and perfecting flavor combinations.

Aside from cooking, I enjoy spending time with my family, fishing and jazz music. It's impossible to choose one favorite ingredient, as there are far too many wonderful options that change with the seasons. Quality and fresh ingredients with a personal touch are what make a dish, which is why the Homemade Ham en Croute 'Papa Jo' embodies my cooking philosophy perfectly. Growing up, my father loved to cook meat and on the weekends he especially loved to create country food dishes, so this ham was a regular accompaniment. To this day, 'Papa Jo' symbolizes love, cherished memories, and exquisite cuisine.

Chefs tip:
This is a perfect Summer dish to enjoy on your patio at night. Serve with Alsace Pinot Blanc.

HAM EN CROUTE 'PAPA JO'
AND FINGERLING POTATO SALAD

BY JEAN JOHO

serves 10

ingredients

ham en croute:

4 lb	rustic bread dough, kept cold
flour, as needed	
3 lb	lightly smoked cooked boneless country ham
1 cup	water

potato salad:

2 lb	fingerling potatoes
2 tbsp	diced double smoked bacon
1	shallot, chopped
1	garlic clove, chopped
½ cup	melfor vinegar
½ cup	chicken stock
½ cup	Pinot Blanc
1 tsp	Dijon mustard
salt & pepper, to taste	
parsley, chopped	

to serve:

horseradish sauce
Dijon mustard

method

ham en croute:

Roll out the dough on a floured table to 1" thickness and wrap the ham in the dough. Carefully close any openings. Set aside on a baking tray in a warm area and leave to rise.

Preheat the oven to 550°F. Insert the tray with the ham in the oven and spray (using a spray bottle) the water over to create steam, then close the door quickly. Cook for 15 minutes and then lower the temperature to 325°F and bake for 1 hour and 30 minutes or until the ham is warmed through.

potato salad:

Steam the potatoes, and when they are done (they should be tender when pierced with a fork), remove from the heat and gently peel. Set aside for 15 minutes to cool, then slice into a salad bowl. In a hot skillet, add and fry the bacon until golden brown.

Add the shallot and garlic clove. Deglaze with the vinegar, chicken stock and Pinot Blanc. Add the Dijon mustard and bring all the ingredients to a boil. Pour over the sliced potatoes. Season with salt and pepper and mix well. Set aside at room temperature for 30 minutes. Garnish with the parsley.

to serve:

Present the whole ham on a cutting board and carve using a serrated knife.

Serve with the fingerling potato salad, horseradish sauce and Dijon mustard.

ROASTED MILK-FED POUSSIN
WITH GUANCIALE, CARAMELIZED BRUSSELS SPROUTS, EXTRA VIRGIN OLIVE OIL POTATO PUREE, CHICKEN JUS

BY JUSTIN ERMINI

This dish is the perfect comfort food. The rich flavor of the poussin is beautifully paired with the sweetness of the caramelized Brussels sprouts. It's a great dish to impress dinner guests.

JUSTIN ERMINI

I was born in Waterbury, Connecticut and grew up in an Italian and Portuguese neighborhood. At 17 I went to The CIA culinary school and I have been traveling ever since. So far I have lived in San Francisco, New Orleans, Los Angeles, New York and even Vermont. I am currently engaged to Mayra Victoria who is a Pastry Chef and we will be getting married in the near future. Currently I live in Washington, Connecticut in a small farm town in Litchfield county. It's very different from living in the city but I am really starting to enjoy it.

I guess traveling and eating would be my main hobbies but I also enjoy reading about past culinary greats such as Ferdinand Point (one of my favorites). My favorite spice is definitely coriander seed and I also enjoy the Litchfield county area for ingredients such as fresh milk from Arethusa Farm and beef, pork and chicken from Greyledge Farm. We pick our own heirloom tomatoes at Waldingfield Farm and I love working with local purveyors and being hands on with the farmers.

"a great dish to impress dinner guests"

184

ROASTED MILK-FED POUSSIN
WITH GUANCIALE, CARAMELIZED BRUSSELS SPROUTS, EXTRA VIRGIN OLIVE OIL POTATO PUREE, CHICKEN JUS

BY JUSTIN ERMINI

serves 4

ingredients

poussin:

4	milk-fed poussin
1	carrot, diced
2	celery stalks, diced
¼ cup	garlic
1	lemon
1	sprig of thyme, chopped
	bay leaves
	butter, as needed
	sea salt & white pepper, to taste

extra virgin olive oil potato purée: (yields 4 cups)

12	creamer potatoes, peeled
16 cups	water
3 tbsp	salt
¼ cup	butter, kept cold
1 cup	heavy cream, hot
¼ cup	extra virgin olive oil
¼ cup	chives, chopped fine
	sea salt & white pepper, to taste

caramelized Brussels sprouts: (yields 1 qt)

12	Brussels sprouts
¼ cup	olive oil
1 cup	guanciale, sliced thin and diced
	sea salt & pepper, to taste
2 tbsp	tarragon, chopped

to serve:

4 cups	potato purée
4 cups	caramelized Brussels sprouts with guanciale
1 cup	chicken jus

method

poussin:

Stuff the carcass of each poussin with carrot, celery, garlic, ¼ lemon, thyme and bay leaf. Truss the poussin, and rub with butter, salt and pepper. Roast at 375°F in a fan oven for 25 minutes. Set aside the chicken jus for serving.

potato purée:

Add the potatoes and salt to the water and simmer slowly for about 20 minutes. Drain the potatoes and let dry for 5 minutes. Put the potatoes through a food mill with the cold butter, fold in the hot cream, add the olive oil and chives and re-season with salt and white pepper.

caramelized Brussels sprouts:

Trim the bottoms off the Brussels sprouts and cut them in half. Blanch in salted boiling water for 5 minutes and shock in ice water. Bring a large sauteuse with olive oil to a medium to high heat. Place the Brussels sprouts in face down and cook until golden brown. Drain off the excess oil and add guanciale to the pan. Season with salt and pepper to taste and add the tarragon.

to serve:

Serve the poussin in individual dishes with the caramelized Brussels sprouts, potato purée and chicken jus.

On our menu we describe this as 'Nick's Famous Chili'. Nick Kormanik has been working at Triple Creek Ranch for 15 years now. He is a true staple in the kitchen and so is his chili. Our guests and staff enjoy this all year round.

TRIPLE CREEK
MONTANAN CHILI
BY NICK KORMANIK

JACOB LEATHERMAN

I was born and raised in Cincinnati, Ohio and found my interest in food while I was a student at Ohio State University after which I worked in many French restaurants in Cincinnati. Since then I decided to move to Relais & Châteaux in the Rockies and have never looked back!

My favorite ingredient is probably wild game. I especially like locally sustainable ingredients – anything to help out local growers. We grow our own vegetables on the ranch so I'm a big believer in locally produced ingredients. I love the outdoors of the Rockies and my hobbies include fly fishing, hiking, snowshoeing and listening to good music!

I have chosen this dish together with my Sous Chef Nick Kormanik. He has been with Triple Creek Ranch for 15 years and this is his recipe. It has been served at Triple Creek Ranch for over 10 years and is very popular at lunchtime!

"we grow our own vegetables on the ranch"

TRIPLE CREEK MONTANAN CHILI

BY NICK KORMANIK

serves 12

ingredients

½	onion, diced
½	red pepper, diced
½	green pepper, diced
½	yellow pepper, diced
2 tbsp	garlic, chopped
½ tbsp	granulated garlic
¾ lb	prime rib, venison or tenderloin trim, cubed
1	27 oz can tomatoes, diced
1	27 oz can kidney beans
½ tbsp	paprika
1½ tbsp	chili powder
½ tbsp	salt
½ tbsp	black pepper
½ cup	chili sauce

method

Sauté together the onions, peppers and garlic. Add the meat, tomatoes and beans, then add the seasonings. Bring to the boil then simmer for at least 2 hours, add water when necessary.

to serve:

Simply serve in a bowl and enjoy with accompaniments of your choice.

Chef's tip:
Don't be afraid to season the chili to your taste, it's good to experiment!

SOPHISTICATED KOBE BURGER

BY DAVID DANIELS

Our sophisticated Kobe Burger has been a crowd favorite since its inception.

DAVID DANIELS

I have always lived by one mantra: passion perseveres. My career has led me on a road trip of a lifetime across the country to some of the finest restaurants in order to gain invaluable hands-on experience. I moved back to my native New England to Nantucket and joined the very polished staff at The Wauwinet, where I am now Executive Chef.

I now call The Wauwinet and Nantucket Island my home. My hobbies include traveling, physical fitness and spending as much time as possible with my two kids, David and Olivia. My family plays a very important role in my cooking style and my grandmother and mother have always been supportive in both maintaining and influencing traditions and quality.

Chef's tip:
Let the burgers rest for 3 minutes after searing to seal in the juices.

SOPHISTICATED KOBE BURGER

BY DAVID DANIELS

serves 4

ingredients	method

burger:

2 lb	ground Kobe beef or ground sirloin
8 tbsp	caramelized onions
1 tbsp	chopped capers
1 tsp	sambal
1 tsp	Dijon mustard
salt & black pepper	

truffled French fries:

3	large russet potatoes
½ gallon	canola oil
4 tbsp	grated parmesan
2 tbsp	truffle oil
1 tbsp	chopped Italian flat parsley
salt	

lettuce, tomatoes and onions (LTO) and pickles:

4	pieces hydroponic Bibb lettuce
4	slices vine ripe tomatoes
4	slices red onions
4	slices pickles
4	brioche rolls

burger:

Chop the caramelized onions finely then mix with the capers. Mix the ground Kobe beef/sirloin with the onions and capers. Add the remaining ingredients to the mixture, form into four 8 oz burgers and set aside. Heat a cast iron pan on medium high heat. Season the burgers on both sides with salt and black pepper. Add to the cast iron pan and sear for 3 minutes on both sides to obtain medium rare (add an additional minute for medium, medium well and well done on both sides).

truffled French fries:

Cut the potatoes lengthwise ⅛"x ⅛". Heat the canola oil to 110°F. Add the fries to the oil and cook for 3 minutes. Remove and cool to room temperature. Heat the oil to 150°F, add the fries and cook until crisp (approximately 8 minutes). Remove from the oil and place in a large bowl. Toss the fries thoroughly with the remaining ingredients.

to serve:

Place a brioche roll on a plate and place lettuce, tomatoes, onions (LTO) and pickles on top of the bun as desired. Place the burger on top of the LTO. Serve the fries alongside the burger in a bowl.

BAKED STUFFED GARLIC CHICKEN
WITH JASMINE RICE AND BABY SPINACH

BY GRAHAM GILL

This is a favorite home dish of mine that is easy to prepare and always proves to be a winner. The garlic cream cheese and herbs are a great combination and add a quick injection of flavor to a regular chicken dinner.

GRAHAM GILL

I was born in Bromley, Kent in England and relocated to America in 1982 after spending two years in Bermuda. I now live locally in Vermont in the town of Brattleboro. I have two children, a son and a daughter, both in their twenties.

I am spoilt for choice when it comes to the abundant, top quality local ingredients that can be found in Vermont; but a particular favorite of mine has always been the beautiful Vermont venison.

When I'm not in the kitchen, I enjoy the outdoors and fishing in the local rivers.

This dish was first created at home simply by combining larder staple supplies that needed using up. My wife's love of garlic and cream cheese was the inspiration and I decided to liven up a plain chicken breast by mixing the two together and stuffing the chicken with it. Flour, egg and breadcrumbs were added to help keep the stuffed chicken breast together – it has proven to be a winner with the family ever since!

BAKED STUFFED GARLIC CHICKEN
WITH JASMINE RICE AND BABY SPINACH

BY GRAHAM GILL

serves 4

ingredients

chicken:

4	chicken breasts (skinless), 6-7 oz
8 oz	cream cheese (not whipped)
2-3	cloves garlic, finely chopped
1 tsp	chopped fresh mixed herbs eg. thyme, tarragon, parsley
½ cup	plain flour for dredging
2	eggs, beaten
¼ cup	whole milk
2 cups	Panko breadcrumbs or seasoned Italian breadcrumbs
	salt & pepper
	drizzle of olive oil

jasmine rice:

1 cup	jasmine rice
4 cups	water
	salt & pepper

to serve:

10 oz	baby spinach, washed thoroughly under cold water and drained
1 tbsp	olive oil
	salt & pepper

Chefs tip:

Use fresh herbs wherever possible when cooking, it makes a real difference to the flavor you will achieve. It is worth the extra price! If you have any leftover filling you can warm it and swirl it across the plate.

method

chicken:

Lay the chicken breasts skinless side down on a cutting board. In order to stuff the breast you first have to make one large pocket to hold the cream cheese. To do this you need to make two cuts by running a knife down the center of the breast slicing towards the outside (being careful not to cut through the edge); repeat the process for both sides, leaving the breast with two flaps that open.

In a bowl mix the cream cheese, herbs and garlic. Add 2 oz of the filling to the pocket, and fold back the flaps so the breast looks whole again.

Take three small plates and add seasoned flour to one, eggs to another and breadcrumbs to a third. Place the chicken breast in the flour, followed by the eggs and breadcrumbs, always coating on all sides.

jasmine rice:

In a pan bring the water to the boil, add the rice and season. Bring to the boil and then simmer until the rice is tender, approximately 10 minutes, stirring occasionally.

to serve:

Preheat the oven to 350°F. Heat a cast iron frying pan or ovenproof skillet until hot. Drizzle with olive oil. Place the chicken breasts skin down and cook until the breadcrumbs start to color. Place in a preheated oven at 350°F for 10 minutes. Turn the breasts over and return to the oven for another 8-10 minutes, until the cream cheese starts to leak out. Remove from the oven and allow to rest. At the last minute heat a pan on the stove with a tablespoon of olive oil, drop in the spinach and toss over the heat for 2-3 minutes until wilted, then season. Place a metal ring on the plate at the front center and three-quarters fill with rice. Fill the remainder with spinach, then remove the ring. Halve the chicken and rest it on the rice and spinach with the cream cheese facing the front.

PAN ROASTED CAROLINA QUAIL
WITH SWEET POTATO AND LEEK RAGOUT

BY ROBERT CARTER

Quail is an indigenous game bird of South Carolina ... many plantation owners still have quail hunts today. The bird is moist if cooked correctly and eats like dark meat. Pan roasted and stuffed it is a very elegant first course or entrée.

ROBERT CARTER

I currently reside in Mount Pleasant with my wife of over nine years and two kids, Benjamin and Harrison. Originally from the Florida Panhandle, I attended Johnson and Wales University in Charleston and previously served as Executive Chef at Blackberry Farm, Marquesa Hotel, Blue Ridge Grill and Richmond Hill Inn. When I'm not overseeing the kitchen at Peninsula Grill, I enjoy family time riding bikes, boating, visiting local farmers' markets and playing with Halsey, our family's 13-year-old Golden Retriever. At home, I enjoy cooking with my family using ingredients from the ocean's bounty, including local oysters, stone crab claws and triggerfish.

Chef's tip:
Ask your butcher to prepare the quails for you.

PAN ROASTED CAROLINA QUAIL
WITH SWEET POTATO AND LEEK RAGOUT

BY ROBERT CARTER

serves 6 as an appetizer
3 as an entrée

ingredients

quails:

6	quails, prepared for stuffing
¼ cup	onion, brunoise
¼ cup	celery, brunoise
1 cup	cornbread
1 cup	pecans, toasted
¼ cup	butter, melted
1 cup	chicken stock
salt & pepper	

sweet potato and leek ragout:

1 tbsp	butter
2 tbsp	shallots
1 tbsp	garlic
2 cups	sweet potatoes, cut into ¼" dice
2 cups	leeks, cut into ¼" dice
1½ cups	heavy cream
½ cup	chicken stock
salt & pepper	

method

quails:

Sweat the onion and celery together in some butter until translucent. Combine with the cornbread, pecans and melted butter. Pour in enough chicken stock to bind all the ingredients so that the stuffing can be formed into balls and hold their shape. Stuff each quail (approximately 1½ tablespoons per quail) and season.

sweet potato and leek ragout:

Combine the butter, shallots and garlic, and sweat over a low heat. Add the sweet potatoes and leeks, and sauté for 2 minutes. Add the heavy cream and chicken stock and reduce by half. Adjust the seasoning to taste.

to serve:

Preheat the oven to 450°F. Sear the quails, breast side down, until golden. Turn the quails and place in the oven. Cook for 5-7 minutes or until cooked as desired. Evenly distribute the ragout into six (or three) pasta-style bowls, set a quail on top of the ragout and serve immediately. Enjoy!

SAUTEED ALBERTA FREE RANGE CHICKEN BREAST

IN ITS OWN JUS WITH MOREL MUSHROOMS, PEARL ONIONS, SMOKED BACON AND SAFFRON RISOTTO

BY HANS SAUTER

Good comfort food. Tasty and pleasing for mostly everyone.

HANS SAUTER

I have two children, a boy and a girl, who live with their mother in Osaka, Japan. I grew up in the village of Küblis located in the Canton of Grison, Switzerland although I have lived all over. My career has been quite international and includes Japan, Hungary, Canada and the United States.

I have chosen this dish as the ingredients are easily available and chicken is tasty and a good comfort food. Plus chicken pleases most people, I meet very few who do not like chicken! I always try to be creative with fresh market cuisine and hopefully that is what I am known for.

Chefs tip:

If you have access to excellent chicken stock then purchase it in advance.

Chefs tip:

It's all about the timing of the risotto! It should be served in a liquid type consistency. Buon Appetito!

SAUTEED ALBERTA FREE RANGE CHICKEN BREAST
IN ITS OWN JUS WITH MOREL MUSHROOMS, PEARL ONIONS, SMOKED BACON AND SAFFRON RISOTTO

BY HANS SAUTER
serves 6

ingredients

chicken breasts:

6	chicken breasts, 7 oz each
olive oil	
salt & ground black pepper	

chicken morel sauce:

1 tbsp	grapeseed oil
¾ cup	julienne of smoked bacon
15	pearl onions, blanched and peeled
1¾ oz	dry morel mushrooms
1 cup	dry white wine
6 cups	chicken stock (see below)
salt & ground white pepper	
2 tbsp	unsalted butter

chicken stock:

4 tbsp	grapeseed oil
6½ lb	chicken bones (backs and necks)
1	onion, coarsely chopped
1	carrot, coarsely chopped
½	celery root (celeriac), coarsely chopped
2	bay leaves
3	branches of thyme
3	branches of rosemary
1 tbsp	black peppercorns
2	garlic cloves
½	leek, coarsely chopped
3 cups	dry white wine
6 qt	water

saffron risotto:

3 tbsp	olive oil

method

chicken breasts:

Preheat the oven to 500°F. Season the chicken. Heat the oil in a fry pan. Sear the breasts each side for about 3 minutes. Place in a baking pan and set aside. Finish the chicken in the oven for approximately 15 minutes to coincide with the risotto.

chicken morel sauce:

Heat the grapeseed oil in a large pan. Sauté the smoked bacon, pearl onions and morel mushrooms. Deglaze with white wine, add the stock and simmer until reduced by half. Season and whisk in chunks of butter.

chicken stock:

Preheat the oven to 450°F. Heat the oil in a heavy roasting pan in the oven. When hot add the chicken bones and roast for approximately 45 minutes, stirring occasionally. Lower the oven to 400°F. Add the onion, carrot, celery, bay leaves, thyme, rosemary, and peppercorns. 15 minutes later add the garlic and leek. After 5 minutes, add the white wine. Cook for 10 more minutes, then remove and scrape all the contents into a large pot. Add the remaining water and simmer for 2-3 hours. Skim the fat and foam frequently and add more water if necessary. Remove the bones with a slotted spoon, strain through a chinois and cloth.

saffron risotto:

Heat the olive oil in a pot. Add the onions, sauté

POACHED EGG
IN A RAGOUT OF BACON
AND CHANTERELLE MUSHROOMS

BY C. BARCLAY DODGE

This dish is very comforting to me. Chanterelles remind me of home and eggs are full of soul. Growing up in the mountains of Colorado, I spent the Fall months foraging for mushrooms and other wild bounty. The Rocky Mountain chanterelle is one of the best mushrooms in the world with the color and scent of ripe apricots and pine.

C. BARCLAY DODGE

I'm from Aspen, Colorado, home of the ski slopes. Now I live in Del Mar, California. I have worked in many areas of the United States and in Spain. I have introduced a California Coastal Ranch cuisine inspired by local ingredients. I feel it is important to make sure dishes are carefully designed and created from locally sourced ingredients.

I have chosen this at-home dish because it reminds me of home, Aspen, and I love eggs and mushrooms. This is a rather quick and very satisfying dish that I can make late at night after a long day. Along with a side of thick cut toast, good butter and a glass of wine, this dish hits home. My favorite ingredients are pork, of any kind, star anise – brings great flavor – and, of course, salt. When I'm not at work I like to relax and keep fit with yoga and I love foraging in the wild to see what I can find. It's great finding things that I can cook!

Chef's tip:

I recommend the full ½ lb of bacon so you can snack on the lardons while cooking ... so good. You'll only need half of them for the actual recipe.

POACHED EGG
IN A RAGOUT OF BACON AND CHANTERELLE MUSHROOMS

BY C. BARCLAY DODGE
serves 4

ingredients

bacon lardons:

8 oz   bacon, ¼" thick slice

chanterelles:

8 oz   chanterelle mushrooms, clean and cut into large bite-size pieces
4   cloves of garlic, sliced thin
2   shallots, sliced thin
2 tbsp   oil or butter
1 tbsp   thyme, freshly chopped
4 oz   white wine
salt, to taste

to serve:

4   eggs, poached or Arzak-style
1½ cups   chicken stock
4 oz   butter
salt, to taste
2 tbsp   parsley, chopped for garnish
2 tbsp   chives, minced for garnish

Chefs tip:

In the restaurant we prepare the eggs in the Arzak 'Fleur de Heuvo' style, but at home a simple poach in simmering water with a splash of vinegar and a pinch of salt is my preference.

method

bacon lardons:

Cut the bacon into ¼"x ¼" cuts, forming lardons. In a small pan cook the bacon for a few minutes over a medium flame then put in a 350°F oven for about 10 minutes or until the bacon has rendered a good amount of fat and is slightly caramelized but still chewy. Leave the bacon lardons in the rendered fat and reserve for later use. (You can make these a few days in advance and keep them in the fridge to snack on or add to other recipes.)

chanterelles:

In a sauté pan sweat the garlic and shallots in oil or butter until lightly caramelized and sweet, then add the mushrooms and continue cooking for a few minutes. Add the thyme and white wine, season with salt and put in a 350°F oven for about 10 minutes or until the wine has evaporated and the mushrooms are lightly roasted. Reserve for later use.

All of the previous steps may be executed the day before. Reserve in the refrigerator.

to serve:

Poach the eggs to your liking.

In the meantime, add half the bacon (or to taste), cooked mushrooms and chicken stock to a pan and cook over a high flame until the stock has reduced by half and tightened up. At this point, add the butter and whisk in to emulsify. Check the salt and garnish with the chopped parsley.

Pour the mushrooms equally into four bowls, place the egg in the center of the mushrooms. Garnish with chopped chives, salt over the

An at-home favorite, this dish blends rich foie gras with sweet prunes and sugar beet.

DUCK FOIE GRAS
WITH PRUNES AND SUGAR BEET
BY YVAN LEBRUN

YVAN LEBRUN

My motto is "simplicity and precision" and it seems to have worked for me! I am originally from the little fishing village of Cancale in Brittany and, together with my partner Rolande, we have created one of the best restaurants in North America. My love of food and desire to combine the best of French and Québec cuisines spur me on in the restaurant.

I have chosen this at-home dish because it's pure with lots of different flavors, plus it's tasty, nice to look at and very inviting. My favorite ingredients are real butter with good bread and white ham. To relax I like to read a nice book, cook and sleep!

"it's tasty, nice to look at and very inviting"

DUCK FOIE GRAS
WITH PRUNES AND SUGAR BEET

BY YVAN LEBRUN

serves 4

ingredients

veal juice:

5 lb	veal bones, roasted
8 oz	carrots, cubed
8 oz	onions, thinly sliced
3 oz	celeriac, cubed
3 oz	garlic cloves
½ oz	thyme
2	bay leaves
1 tsp	ground white pepper
4 oz	white mushrooms
20 cups	vegetable juice
8 cups	water
4 cups	white wine
2 oz	olive oil

saffron sauce:

2 cups	reduction of veal juice (see above)
pinch of saffron	
2 oz	sherry
1 oz	sherry vinegar
2 oz	maple syrup
1 oz	unsalted butter

fruit and vegetables:

2	sugar beets
1	lemon, juice
2	black radishes
2	figs, halved
4	damas plums, halved
garlic confit, to taste	
2	kohlrabi, turnip or parsnip
10	red cherry tomatoes
10	yellow cherry tomatoes
2 oz	green beans
4	mustard leaves

poached duck foie gras:

4 cups	reduction of veal juice
4	escalopes of duck foie gras, 2 oz each

to serve:

1 tbsp	fleur de sel of lemon confit (salt and lemon confit, mixed)
garlic flowers, to garnish	

method

veal juice:

This should be prepared the day before.

In a marmite (tall cooking pot), cook the vegetables and herbs with the olive oil, and add the veal bones. Then add the white wine, vegetable juice and water. Cook for 4 hours over a low heat (slowly). Strain the veal juice reduction and reserve 6 cups.

saffron sauce:

In a casserole, boil 2 cups of the veal juice reduction. Add the saffron, sherry, sherry vinegar and maple syrup. Boil for 5 minutes and then add the butter. Remove from the heat and mix. Reserve.

fruit and vegetables:

Clean and cook the sugar beets in lemon juice infused water until tender. Peel and cut into four pieces. Peel and cut the black radish into circles 1″ round and ⅛″ deep.

In a casserole, pour in 2 tablespoons of the saffron sauce and roast the figs for a few minutes. Add the plums, sugar beet, black radish, garlic confit, kohlrabi, tomatoes, green beans and mustard leaves.

poached duck foie gras:

Bring the veal juice to a simmer (160°F), add the escalopes of foie gras and poach for 3 minutes.

to serve:

Divide the vegetables and fruits between four plates. Pour a little sauce around and add some sel de mer of lemon confit. Top with the duck foie gras and garlic flowers. Serve warm.

RABBIT RAGU
WITH PANCETTA
AND OLIVES
BY SUE SCHICKLER

This is great 'comfort food' to me. The ragù goes well with noodles, potato gnocchi or polenta.

SUE SHICKLER

I live in Warren, Vermont and am originally from Cleveland, Ohio, although I haven't lived there since 1972. I chose the rabbit ragù because it's simple to make and to me is a very comforting dish. The flavors are very rich and satisfying.

My favorite ingredient (besides salt) is any type of cured or smoked pork. I think pancetta, prosciutto, quanciale, smoked bacon or other types of cured ham seem to go well with so many things.

My favorite hobbies are traveling and diving, which I don't really get to do often enough. On a day-to-day basis I love hearing new music, finding new wines and cooking for my friends. I know that really sounds dull, but for the most part it really is what I do on my days off!

"it's simple to make and to me is a very comforting dish"

RABBIT RAGU
WITH PANCETTA AND OLIVES
BY SUE SCHICKLER

serves 4-6

ingredients

rabbit ragù with pancetta and olives:

	forelegs and hind legs from one rabbit. Reserve the loins for another dish, and brown the carcass to make stock.
¼ cup	extra virgin olive oil
4 oz	pancetta, cut into ½" cubes
1	medium onion, small diced
2	cloves garlic, minced
	pinch of Aleppo pepper, or a small pinch of red pepper flakes
1 cup	dry white wine
1	28 oz can tomatoes, preferably San Marzano, cut into cubes
3 cups	rabbit stock or chicken stock
2 tbsp	tarragon, chopped
1 tbsp	parsley, chopped
¼ cup	green olives, Castelvetrano or Picholine, sliced

gremolata:

1	lemon
2 tbsp	parsley, chopped
1	clove garlic, finely minced

to serve:

1	package imported pappardelle, 8 oz
2 tbsp	unsalted butter, cubed
	noodles, gnocchi or polenta, cooked

method

gremolata:

Remove the zest from the lemon using a peeler, being careful to not get any of the white pith. Mince finely, then add the parsley and garlic and continue mincing together until everything is combined and very finely minced.

rabbit ragù with pancetta and olives:

In a large sauce pot heat the olive oil over a medium heat and add the pancetta. Cook, stirring occasionally, until the pancetta is starting to brown nicely but not overly crisp. Remove the pancetta and set aside. Add the onion, garlic and Aleppo/red pepper flakes to the pan and cook for a few minutes to soften but not brown the vegetables. Increase the heat to medium high and add the wine. Cook until most of the wine has evaporated then add the rabbit legs, tomatoes and enough stock to barely cover the legs. Season with salt to taste and bring to a simmer.

Reduce the heat to a slow simmer and simmer gently for 45 minutes, or until the meat is tender and pulls away easily from the bones. Remove the legs and set aside to cool. Taste the ragù, and simmer longer to reduce if it is not flavorful. When the legs are cool enough to handle, pull the meat off the bones and add to the ragù. Add the tarragon, parsley, pancetta and olives.

to serve:

Cook the pappardelle in salted boiling water. Drain and toss with butter in a serving bowl. Add the ragù, combine with the noodles, gnocchi or polenta and divide into four to six bowls. Top with gremolata.

PASTA CARBONARA STYLE

BY MARK LEVY

Great comfort food.

MARK LEVY

I'm currently living the American dream in Saranac Lake upstate New York, although originally I'm from a small town called Stanford-le-Hope in the county of Essex, in the south east of England. This home cook dish has been a favorite of mine since my college days. Back then it was made with any old bacon, button mushrooms and a pack of dried pasta. Today the luxurious pancetta, wild mushroom and handmade pasta version is definitely book-worthy.

I have a number of favorite ingredients but if I was pushed to name only one it would have to be the white truffle. With its mysterious aroma, short availability and extremely high price — it truly is a gem that shouldn't be missed.

My hobbies include dining in New York City when I get a chance, enjoying the peace of the Adirondacks, golfing when there is no snow which isn't too often and living the simple life.

"luxurious pancetta, wild mushroom and handmade pasta"

PASTA CARBONARA STYLE

BY MARK LEVY

serves 4

ingredients

6 oz	pancetta lardons
2	portabella mushrooms
½ cup	dry white wine
1 cup	heavy cream

to serve:

1 lb	fresh noodles
1 tbsp	chopped parsley
4	egg yolks
½ cup	parmesan cheese
salt & pepper	

method

Blanch the lardons to remove some of the saltiness, then sauté with the mushrooms in a large pan until lightly caramelized. Add the wine and reduce by half, then add the cream and boil for about a minute.

to serve:

Boil the noodles until soft then add hot to the bacon mixture. Finish with the chopped parsley, toss well and serve in four bowls, top each with an egg yolk and parmesan cheese. Season to taste and serve immediately.

DESSERTS

Whether it is heavenly chocolate mousse or a melt-in-the-mouth slice of pie, dessert is always a talking point of the meal. This section of the book offers great desserts with a twist – a classic favorite or artisanal dessert with the 'wow factor!'; this selection can tempt any taste bud.

Grand Chef Patrick O'Connell offers the ultimate in baking with his unique 'Apple Tart with Cheddar Cheese Ice Cream'. Imagine yourself in lush tropical islands with Jean-Claude Dufour's 'Litchi and Pink Grapefruit Temptation' or indulge your dark side with Chef Elwyn Boyles' indulgent 'Zeppoles'.

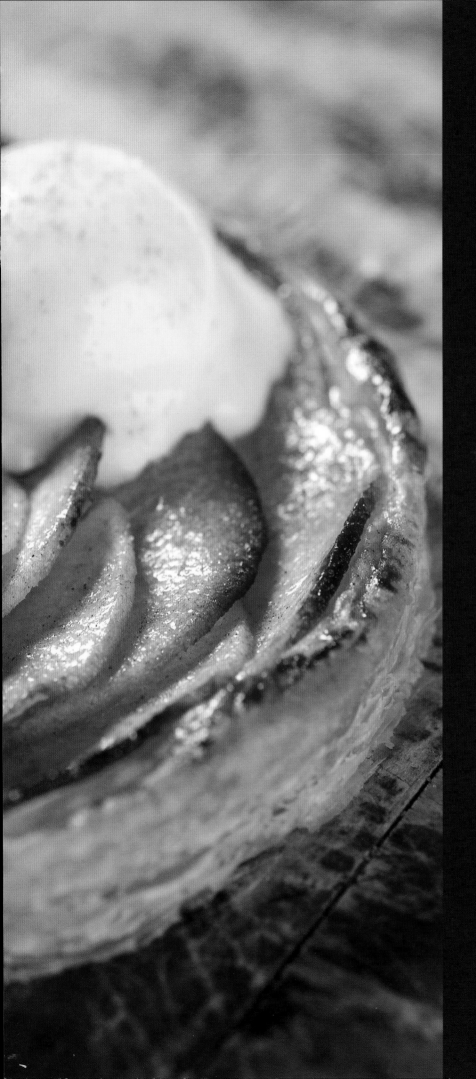

WARM GRANNY SMITH APPLE TART
WITH CHEDDAR CHEESE ICE CREAM

BY PATRICK O'CONNELL

This is the most delicate of apple tarts. Apple slices are sautéed briefly in butter, whiskey and cream, then arranged on thin circles of pastry and baked just before serving. A scoop of Cheddar cheese ice cream melting on top makes them even more irresistible. The tarts can be assembled well in advance, refrigerated and baked just before serving.

PATRICK O'CONNELL

I was born in Washington DC and now live in Washington VA just a stone's throw from The Inn at Little Washington.

I have chosen this recipe as being in the heart of apple-growing country, we've tried every apple dessert imaginable over the years – and this is one of the best.

My favorite ingredients are eggs – I can't live without them. Any hobbies I have are eventually turned into work!

Chefs tip:
Any good Bourbon can be substituted in place of the Southern Comfort.

"we've tried every apple dessert imaginable over the years – and this is one of the best"

WARM GRANNY SMITH APPLE TART
WITH CHEDDAR CHEESE ICE CREAM

BY PATRICK O'CONNELL
serves 6

ingredients

apple tart:

	your favorite pie, croissant or puff pastry dough
2	Granny Smith apples, peeled and cored
3 tbsp	unsalted butter
½ tsp	ground cinnamon
2 tbsp	heavy cream
6 tbsp	Southern Comfort
⅓ cup	sugar mixed with 1 rounded tsp cinnamon

Cheddar cheese ice cream:
(yields 1 qt, 6-8 portions)

1 cup	half and half
1 cup	milk
⅔ cup	sugar
	freshly ground white pepper, to taste
½	vanilla bean, split lengthwise
5	egg yolks
2½ cups	shredded mild Cheddar cheese

Chefs tip:
A mandoline is an ideal way to slice apples quickly and evenly.

method

apple tart:

Preheat the oven to 400°F. On a floured board, roll the dough out to about ⅛" thick. Lay a 5" diameter bowl upside down on the dough and cut out six circles. Place the pastry rounds between sheets of waxed paper and refrigerate.

Using a sharp knife, slice the apples into ⅛" sections. In a large sauté pan, melt the butter over a medium heat. Add the apples and cook for several minutes. Add the cinnamon and cream. Carefully add the Southern Comfort, averting your face, as it will ignite. Continue cooking until the apples are soft and pliable. Remove the apples with a slotted spoon and place on a non-reactive baking sheet, then cool. Simmer the cooking liquid until it is reduced by half.

Spray several baking sheets with non-stick cooking spray and lay the chilled rounds on them. Place the chilled apple slices in concentric circles around the pastry, leaving a ¼" border at the edges. Roll one apple slice into a tight circle to form a 'rosette' and place in the center of each tart. Dust with the cinnamon sugar and bake for 7 minutes, or until golden brown.

Cheddar cheese ice cream:

Combine the half and half, milk, ⅓ cup of sugar, white pepper and vanilla bean. Bring to a boil and remove from the heat. Allow to steep for 5 minutes, then remove the vanilla bean.

Whisk the egg yolks and remaining sugar together until thick and foamy. Slowly pour the half and half mixture into the yolk mixture, whisking vigorously until thoroughly incorporated.

Set the bowl over a pot of simmering water and cook, whisking constantly, until the mixture coats the back of a spoon. Remove from the heat and whisk in the cheese. Strain to remove any lumps. Cool in the refrigerator, then freeze in an ice cream maker.

to serve:

Serve the tart with a scoop of ice cream on top.

WHITE CHOCOLATE AND COCONUT MOUSSE

BY BRIAN PORTEUS

This is a fairly simple but elegant way to end a meal and it works for all seasons. The coconut and chocolate balance well together to provide a unique dessert.

BRIAN PORTEUS

I am from Kilkenny City, Ireland. I have worked in restaurants, hotels and for cruise liners. My cooking style is modern French and I always try to use local ingredients.

My favorite ingredient? While in Europe it would be game. I look forward to when the Fall/Winter season approaches, and the wild fresh variety of game that is available. Outside Europe, in the warmer countries it would be fresh seafood for the varieties that are available, the flavors, the sweetness of the flesh, and the simplicity in using this product. Because of my career, I have traveled extensively around most parts of the world. I enjoy researching projects, improvement thinking and visionary reading. I have a keen interest in astronomy, am a member of the local fitness and health club, and regularly run in mini-marathons for charities. I am a big fan of the Irish Rugby team.

COBBLERS COVE
BARBADOS
Brian Porteus
Executive Chef
RELAIS &
CHATEAUX

"this is a fairly simple but elegant way to end a meal and it works for all seasons"

WHITE CHOCOLATE AND COCONUT MOUSSE

BY BRIAN PORTEUS

serves 12

ingredients

2 oz	coconut liquor
1 tbsp	powdered gelatin
16 oz	heavy cream
8 oz	white chocolate

to serve:

toasted coconut, as needed
sugar, as needed
water, as needed
1   drop of blue food coloring

method

Bloom (soften) the gelatin in cold water. Whip the heavy cream to soft peaks, and melt the chocolate. Heat the coconut liquor and dissolve the gelatin into it. Whisk into the melted chocolate, then whisk in two-thirds of the heavy cream; gently fold in the remaining cream. Pour into serving dishes and refrigerate for at least 3 hours before serving.

to serve:

Sprinkle the toasted coconut in the glass, to create layers of mousse and coconut. For the bubble sugar decoration, mix 2 parts sugar with 1 part water, heat on a low heat until it is reduced to a syrup. Add the blue food coloring and pour onto a sheet tray to cool. When cooled break off into pieces and decorate accordingly.

Chef's tip:
I would recommend using a semi-sweet chocolate for Winter/Fall and the white chocolate for Summer and Spring.

WARM MANGO TART

BY AARON WRATTEN

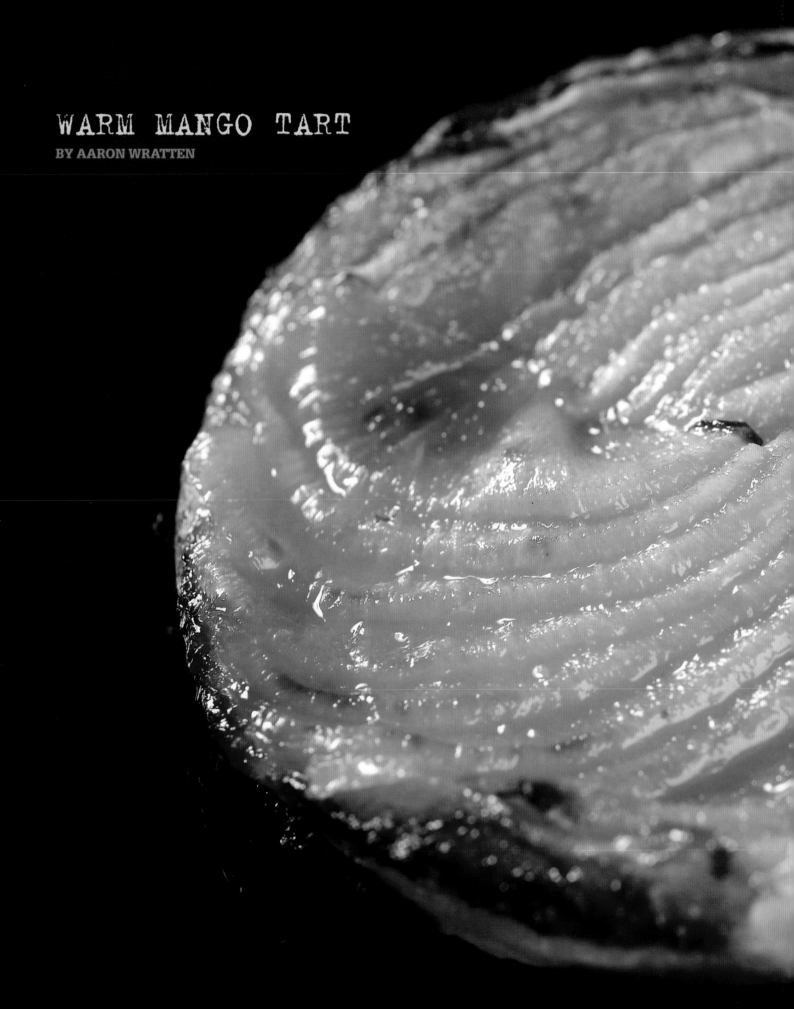

These are fairly simple to make. The trick is slicing the mangos very thinly and arranging them nicely on the puff pastry. You don't need all the mango paste for the tarts, but it's very good on bread in the morning too.

AARON WRATTEN

I grew up in a restaurant on a farm, in the middle of New York State. My family grew vegetables and raised Horned Dorset sheep, tended to an apple orchard, bees, pheasants and hops. The restaurant in Leonardsville is still the other focus of our lives and home.

This is an elegant dessert, yet fairly quick to prepare and there's a great satisfaction in preparing things from your own back yard. It makes them taste that much better!

Favorite ingredient? I would cherish anything with integrity, that is the best it can be, that tastes of itself and of its origin. Right now, I'm thinking of a carrot.

In our spare time my wife Maddalena and I travel when we can, especially to her native Italy. I enjoy music and films plus days off just enjoying our home.

Chefs tip:

Make the mango paste first, or even days in advance.

"this is an elegant dessert, yet fairly quick to prepare"

WARM MANGO TART

BY AARON WRATTEN

serves 4

ingredients

mango tart:

puff pastry, enough to make four 6″ circles

2	large mangos, peeled and cut as close to the pit as possible
4 tbsp	mango paste (see below)
2 tbsp	sugar, for sprinkling

vanilla ice cream (optional)

mango paste: (makes 2 cups)

2 cups	mangos, peeled and roughly chopped
½ tsp	orange, zest
1	orange, juice
½ cup	Turbinado or light brown sugar
1	small cinnamon stick

to serve:

vanilla ice cream (optional)

Chef's tip:

If lifting the mango 'circle' fails, simply place the slices one by one in the form of a fan until you get all the way around.

method

mango paste:

Combine the mango, the zest and the orange juice in a blender to make a fine purée. Place in a small pan with the sugar and cinnamon stick. Simmer, stirring frequently, until reduced by about a third, amber in color and jelly-like in consistency. Remove the cinnamon and store covered in the refrigerator for up to a week.

mango tart:

Preheat the oven to 450°F. Lay the puff pastry sheets on a lightly floured surface and dust lightly with flour. Roll to ⅛″ if necessary. Cut four 6″ circles from the pastry using a coffee saucer and a sharp knife. Place the circles on a lightly greased cookie sheet.

Cut the mangos to make four fillets. If the fillets are more than 3″ wide trim off the excess. Trim off the remaining flesh, if any, from the pit and chop into small pieces. Using a very sharp knife or a good serrated knife, slice the fillets (flat side down) across as thinly as possible. Try to keep them together like a deck of cards.

Bring the mango paste to room temperature and stir so that it is the consistency of jelly but not liquid, adding drops of water if necessary. Place a spoonful of mango paste in the middle of each pastry circle. Spread evenly as for a pizza. Place a spoonful of chopped mango in the centers if you have any.

Gently fan the mango fillets out: pushing them with cupped hands, form the slices around into a circle, the same size as the pastry. With a wide spatula carefully pick up the circle and place it atop the pastry. Sprinkle lightly with sugar. If possible place the tray on a second empty tray (this will help prevent burning on the bottom). Place in the oven. After 5 minutes, when things begin to bubble, lower the oven to 350°F. Remove as soon as the edges begin to puff and brown, being careful that they do not burn on the bottom.

to serve:

Serve the tart warm with vanilla ice cream.

POACHED PEAR
AND HAZELNUT
FRANGIPANE TARTLET
BY KOSTA STAICOFF

This is a combination of some of the most memorable ingredients that I grew up with in the Rogue Valley of southern Oregon. Served warm or cold, for an indulgent breakfast or rustic dessert, this one reminds me of being a kid.

KOSTA STAICOFF

I live and work most of the year in Nevis, a little island in the West Indies. It's a lovely place that really exemplifies the Caribbean lifestyle. My home is in southern Oregon though. That's where I most feel myself and in my spare time my hobbies are snorkeling, foraging and white water rafting. I take inspiration from the ingredients themselves, and the people who raise them. Walking through an open market talking with farmers and ranchers leaves me brimming with ideas to explore.

In cooking I try to recreate a moment that is special to me and give it to someone else. Try and take the time to look and really see — the veins in that pear, or the eye of that tuna loin. That's what drives me to give it the respect it deserves. For my favorite ingredient as part of a recipe, I would have to say salt. But my favorite thing to cook with and eat is probably a freshly foraged wild chanterelle.

Chef's tip:
To prepare larger quantities of the pears submerge each after peeling in water and lemon juice before poaching.

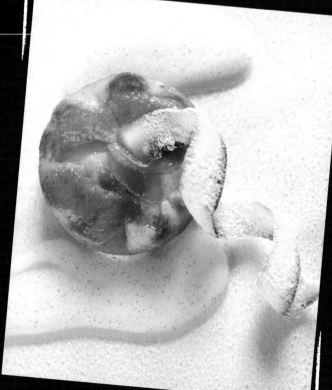

POACHED PEAR
AND HAZELNUT FRANGIPANE TARTLET

BY KOSTA STAICOFF

serves 6

ingredients

poached pears:

3	ripe bartlett pears
4 cups	water
1 cup	white wine
8 oz	sugar
1	cinnamon stick
½	lemon, juice and zest
½	orange, juice and zest

sugar paste:

1 cup	all purpose flour
1 cup	butter
¾ cup	icing sugar
sea salt, to taste	
4	egg yolks

hazelnut frangipane:

½ cup	butter
½ cup	sugar
1 tbsp	flour
½ cup	roasted, finely ground hazelnuts
1 tsp	vanilla extract
2	egg yolks

tuile spiral:

2 oz	butter, softened
2 oz	icing sugar
3 oz	all purpose flour
3	egg whites

vanilla froth:

1 cup	fat free milk
1½ oz	sugar
½	vanilla pod, scraped

Chef's tip:

The sugar paste keeps well for several days in the fridge and can be frozen.

method

poached pears:

Bring all the ingredients except the pears to a boil for a syrup and reduce the heat to a simmer. Peel the pears and add quickly and carefully. Ensure they are covered and poach for 20 minutes, turning them every few minutes. Remove and allow to cool in the syrup.

sugar paste:

Sift the flour and combine with the butter, add the sugar and salt. Add the egg yolks and combine. Work the dough in by hand until smooth then wrap and refrigerate for 1 hour.

hazelnut frangipane:

Beat the butter and the sugar together until light in texture. Combine the flour, hazelnuts and vanilla and add one-third to the butter/sugar, then add one egg yolk and another third of the dry ingredients. When combined, add the second egg yolk and the last of the dry ingredients and mix until fully combined.

tuile spiral:

Preheat the oven to 350°F. Mix the butter, sugar and flour together then slowly add the egg whites until incorporated. Place 1 teaspoon of the mix onto a silpat or parchment paper and with the back of the spoon smooth out evenly to a ½" x 5" rectangle. Bake until light brown, remove from the oven and quickly wrap each one pan side first around the rounded handle of a wooden spoon to form the spiral shape.

vanilla froth:

Using a hand-held mixer, blend all the ingredients to a froth.

to serve:

Lightly butter 3¾" tartlet tins. Roll out the sugar paste to ⅛" thick. Using a round pastry cutter, cut circles slightly bigger than the tins and line them. Place onto a baking tray and fill one-third with frangipane. Halve each pear, remove the stem and seeds, cut into a fan and trim to fit each tartlet. Bake for 20 minutes or until browned. Serve with a tuile spiral and vanilla froth.

EDEN ROCK — ST. BARTHS

LITCHI AND PINK GRAPEFRUIT TEMPTATION

BY JEAN-CLAUDE DUFOUR

Best enjoyed with a glass of pink Champagne, this tantalizing dessert with fresh fruity flavors is the perfect ending to any meal and can be served with a scoop of homemade ice cream.

JEAN-CLAUDE DUFOUR

The girls in my family, Sonia my wife and Thelma our daughter, love creating tempting desserts after a day in the sun, whereas our young boy Marius and I enjoy preparing the fish we catch from our boat. Spending quality time in the kitchen, whether at home or at the Eden Rock, is what I savor most.

We chose this dessert because it's a very colorful dish with fresh ingredients, a little bit like our small island in the Caribbean.

My favorite ingredients are fish of all types, especially tartare or grilled. I also like asparagus, spices and fresh salads. I like to work with various ingredients to create my special sauces, as all sauces are prepared here at the Eden Rock and so 'homemade' is justifiably everywhere within the various menus.

For my hobbies I like sport and fishing and being outside in the open air.

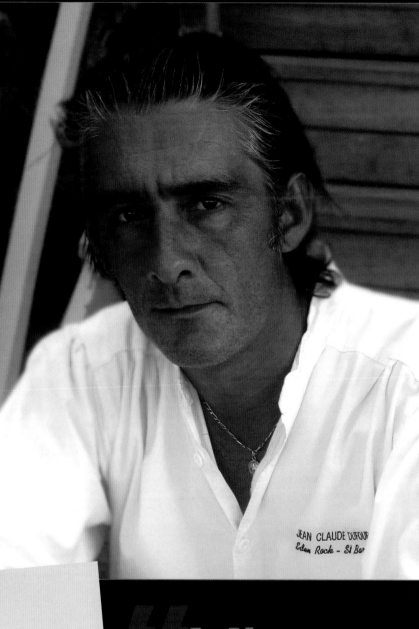

"delicate flavors and romantic shades of pink"

LITCHI AND PINK GRAPEFRUIT TEMPTATION

BY JEAN-CLAUDE DUFOUR

serves 8

ingredients

pastry:

5 oz	soft butter
5 oz	icing sugar
1 tsp	salt
10 oz	flour
2	eggs

litchi ganache:

3½ oz	litchi juice
10 oz	white chocolate
1½ oz	white chocolate for the pie bottom
2	sheets of gelatin, bloomed (softened in cold water)
3½ oz	liquid cream

grapefruit cream:

4½ oz	Chinese grapefruit juice
4	eggs
8	egg yolks
7 oz	caster sugar
8½ oz	butter
2	sheets of gelatin, bloomed

pink icing:

3 oz	water
4½ oz	caster sugar
2	sheets of gelatin, bloomed
red food coloring	

to serve:

homemade ice cream

method

pastry:

Mix the butter and sugar to form a smooth paste. Add the salt, flour and eggs, mixing until the pastry can be shaped into a ball. Place the pastry, covered in plastic, in the fridge for approximately 20 minutes. Roll into a circle large enough to cover a buttered pie form. Return the pie dish to the fridge and leave for 1 hour. Preheat the oven to 400°F. Dock the dough with a fork. Bake in the oven for approximately 20 minutes, until cooked.

litchi ganache:

Melt the 10 oz of white chocolate. Mix the litchi juice and cream together and bring to a quick boil. Mix with the white chocolate and add the softened gelatin. Mix together into a homogeneous cream. Melt the white chocolate and spread onto the pie bottom. Cover the chocolate base with the litchi ganache.

grapefruit cream:

Bring the juice to a quick boil. Whisk the eggs, yolks and sugar together until the sugar is dissolved. Continue to beat the mixture over a bain marie until cooked. Whisk in the butter and add the softened gelatin. Place in the fridge to cool down, then pour on top of the ganache and fill the pie dish nearly up to the top.

pink icing:

Boil the water and sugar for 5 minutes until it becomes syrupy (220°F with a sugar thermometer). Pour the syrup onto the softened gelatin and add a few drops of the red food coloring until the icing becomes a light pink color. Leave the icing to cool down to room temperature (to avoid melting the grapefruit cream, the icing must be cooled down sufficiently). The icing will thicken slightly, making it ideal to cover the pie.

to serve:

Serve with a scoop of homemade ice cream.

Chef's tip:

Crystallized rose petals or a thin layer of white chocolate may be used to decorate the tart.

"there is one word to describe artisanal desserts – heavenly!"

CARIBBEAN 'CHAUDEAU' AND CHURROS

BY STEPHANE MAZIERES

Caribbean specialty that you will also enjoy cooking.

STEPHANE MAZIERES

I'm originally from Rochefort-sur-Mer in the Charente Maritime region of France. It is my French roots that have led me back to Hôtel Le Toiny twice, as I love the French-influenced culture of St. Barts. I have chosen this dish because it is so tasty, churros are well known worldwide and the cream is a specialty of the West Indies, and of course it's full of flavors that will please everyone!

The ingredient which I like to work with the most is fish, it is a delicate and extremely fine product; also great for me, as I live on an island with the catch of the day in proximity. Plus raw or cooked fish is very good for your health.

I am an outdoor fitness enthusiast and an avid scuba diver. I love the lifestyle of the islands, embracing natural flavors and combining them with refined French style which features beautiful plate presentations.

"full of flavors that will please everyone!"

CARIBBEAN 'CHAUDEAU' AND CHURROS

BY STEPHANE MAZIERES

serves 6

ingredients

chaudeau:

2 pt	milk
1	vanilla pod
1	cinnamon stick
1	lime, zest
½ oz	ginger, peeled and grated
1 tsp	orange blossom
4	eggs
4½ oz	caster sugar

churros:

9 oz	milk
3½ oz	butter
1	vanilla pod
a pinch of salt	
7 oz	wheat flour
3	eggs
sugar, as needed	

Chef's tip:

You can use a freezer plastic bag for the churros if you do not have a cuisine piping bag.

method

chaudeau:

Put the milk in a saucepan, and add the vanilla pod cut down the middle, the cinnamon stick, zest of lime, the ginger, and orange blossom. Bring to a boil.

Mix the eggs and the sugar in a bowl, then pour the milk on top through a large strainer. Whip the mixture, pour into a saucepan and cook at a low temperature until the mixture thickens (test the mixture by placing a finger on the mix on the spatula – it has to show a visible print). Store this cream in the fridge. (During cooking, in case the cream accidentally happens to boil or if small deposits appear, remove the saucepan from the heat, pour the mix in a bowl and mix again with a mixer.)

churros:

Put the milk, butter, vanilla pod, and salt together in a saucepan and bring to a boil. Then pour the flour onto the boiling milk and stir constantly with a wooden spatula still on the heat, in order to dry out the dough.

2 minutes later, pour the mixture in a bowl and incorporate the eggs, one by one, until the mix has absorbed them and has become homogeneous. You can either keep it in the fridge for 24 hours or use it immediately.

Put the churros mix in a cuisine piping bag and pour into a deep fryer (340°F to 400°F), making sticks of various shapes, and keep them in the deep fryer until they are golden. Remove and drain on absorbent paper.

to serve:

Sprinkle with sugar, icing sugar or cocoa. In a large plate, place a glass of the 'chaudeau' with a straw in it, and do the same in another glass next to the previous one but with the churros in it. Enjoy dipping hot or cold.

ZEPPOLES

BY ELWYN BOYLES AND
ALESSANDRA ALTIERI

*A great dessert to make at home, very easy
to make and can be prepared in advance.*

ELWYN BOYLES

I am from a small holding in the middle of the Welsh countryside within the United Kingdom. I have been working in the United States for some time now and like to use traditional American ingredients such as popcorn and Sassafras in my desserts. I always aim to make my desserts a pleasure to see as well as to taste.

Together with my Pastry Sous Chef, Alessandra Altieri, we have chosen these zeppoles as they are a great dessert to make at home, very easy to make and can be prepared in advance. My favorite ingredients are strawberries and when I have time off I like to go fishing.

"a great dessert to make at home, very easy to make"

ZEPPOLES

BY ELWYN BOYLES AND ALESSANDRA ALTIERI

makes approximately 50 zeppoles

ingredients	method

zeppoles:

2 cups	water
1 tsp	salt
4 tbsp	light brown sugar
⅓ lb	butter
2 cups	all purpose flour
7	eggs

oil, for frying

granulated sugar, for dusting

Chef's tip:

After cooking, move the zeppoles onto a sheet pan lined with paper towels to soak up any additional excess oil.

zeppoles:

In a medium saucepan, bring the water, salt, sugar, and butter to a boil. Pour in the flour. With a wooden spoon, quickly stir until the mixture starts to come together. Once that begins, turn the heat off and continue to cook in the hot pan until the lumps of flour disappear and the dough begins to form a smooth ball. Pour into a standing mixer fitted with the paddle attachment on very low speed, for about 1 minute, to cool slightly. Slowly start adding the eggs in two at a time, but do not add the next eggs until the previous ones are fully incorporated. Scrape down the bowl occasionally. Continue to mix on very low speed until everything is fully combined. Remove the mixture from the bowl and place into a pastry bag fitted with a #14 star tip.

Fill a medium-sized pot one-third of the way full with oil. Put over a medium heat and hold the oil between 355-365°F. Cut approximately 50 parchment paper squares to 3"x 3". Pipe a 2" doughnut-shaped circle onto one of the individual parchment squares. Pipe the circles on each parchment until there is no more mixture (this might make a little more or a little less than 50 zeppoles, depending on how you pipe). Once everything is piped drop the first zeppole into the oil, parchment side up. Allow it to fry until you just begin to see the edge turn a slight brown, then turn it over. Allow to fry for about 30 seconds then, using tongs, pull the parchment off the bottom of the zeppole and scoop the paper out of the oil, allowing it to continue to fry. It should cook for about 3 minutes in total; flip while frying to ensure even coloring. Continue to keep the oil between 355-365°F. Pull the zeppole out of the oil and place onto a cooling rack to allow the oil to drain off. Dust with granulated sugar.

to serve:

Delicious with ricotta sorbet and chocolate sauce!

MEXICAN CHURROS
BY ALEXIS PALACIOS

These miniature vanilla churros with Cajeta caramel are so delicious you'll keep coming back for more!

ALEXIS PALACIOS

I live in Cabo San Lucas and joined the team at Esperanza Resort in November 2009. Before Esperanza I have worked in Austin, Texas and Dubai. I am originally from Mexico City, and Mexican through and through!

I chose this as my home dish because it really represents Mexico, its something that we eat at home a lot and it uses my favorite ingredient, Mexican Vanilla! Plus its great for kids or when guests come to visit. When I'm not working I enjoy water-sports which Mexico is great for and of course playing basketball.

MEXICAN CHURROS

BY ALEXIS PALACIOS

serves 4

ingredients

churros dough:

1¾ pt	water
1 oz	salt
10 oz	butter
1 lb	flour
10	eggs
vegetable oil, for frying	
2 oz	sugar mixed with cinnamon

Cajeta caramel:

6 oz	sugar
10 oz	milk

method

churros dough:

Boil the water with the salt and butter, add the flour and cook for 15 minutes over a slow heat, working the dough all the time, then allow it to cool down. Put the dough in a mixer and add the eggs one by one. Beat the dough for 10 minutes.

Put the dough in a piping bag, and pipe into churros shapes. Fry them in the oil for approximately 5-8 minutes. Remove and dust with sugar and cinnamon.

Cajeta caramel:

Heat the sugar until it starts to dissolve into a caramel, then add the milk little by little and mix it in. Reduce the mixture to half.

to serve:

Placed the churros on a plate and use the Cajeta caramel as a dipping sauce.

Chefs tip:
Use your favorite ice cream to serve with the churros.

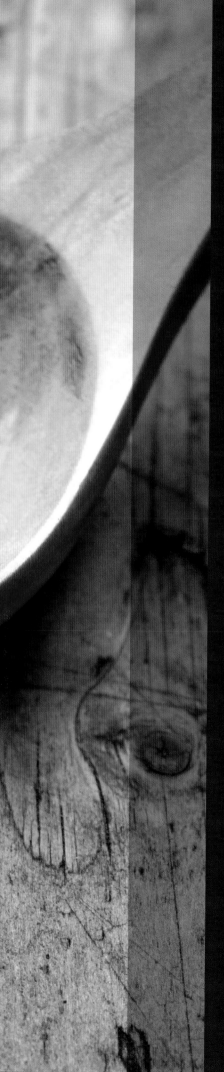

AND FINALLY...

... a few extra treats to really make you feel at home. This selection of baked goods and indulgent extras are great any time of day!

Start your day well with Canoe Bay's traditional Scottish 'Apple-Cinnamon Baked Oatmeal', passed on by Lisa Dobrowolski's father, the perfect dish for a cold Winter morning. Indulge your inner child with Chef Gilles Ballay's 'Trio of Cookies' – certain to be a winner with all the family! Perhaps a simple accompaniment for cheese will catch your eye with Christopher Kostow's 'Port Cherries', the ultimate match for a classic cheese board. These additional recipes are the favorites of our Chefs and their families!

APPLE-CINNAMON BAKED OATMEAL

BY DAN AND LISA DOBROWOLSKI

A perpetual hit with guests, whether at our home or at the hotel. This is a great make-mostly-ahead dish that starts any day of the week off right!

DAN AND LISA DOBROWOLSKI

...e were newly married when we left our
media careers in Chicago to launch
Canoe Bay and we have always blended
home with work. Whenever family
members come to visit, there's no
question that we'll all have dinner
... Canoe Bay's restaurant, but in the
...rning, cooking and sharing breakfast
at home is a special treat.

We've always loved oatmeal for
breakfast — Lisa's dear father, who
...emigrated to the United States from
Scotland, called it porridge. This
...ked version is one of the very first
recipes we served at Canoe Bay.

APPLE-CINNAMON BAKED OATMEAL

BY LISA DOBROWOLSKI

serves 8

ingredients

2 cups	slow-cook oats
1 cup	brown sugar
½ tsp	salt
½ tbsp	ground cinnamon
½ cup	raisins
1 cup	non-fat dry milk
1	Granny Smith apple (or any firm baking apple): cored, peeled, quartered, and sliced in ⅛″ thick wedges
4 cups	boiling water

method

In the morning, preheat the oven to 350°F. Combine all the dry ingredients. Place one heaping cup of the dry oatmeal mix in each of four 15 oz oven-safe bowls. Add one cup of boiling water to each bowl and stir to blend.

Lay the apple slices on top of the oat mixture in each bowl, dividing evenly among four bowls, and press the slices until covered with water. Bake on the center rack, uncovered, for 30–35 minutes, until the oatmeal is set and the apple slices are tender.

to serve:

Present to your sweetheart with a pair of spoons and enjoy, adding more brown sugar and warmed cream as desired.

Chef's tip:
This dry oatmeal mix may be stored for up to two weeks in an airtight container.

263

VIRGIN ISLANDS' COCONUT DROPS

BY JERMAINE GEORGE

serves 4-6

ingredients

1	dry coconut, shelled and grated
3 cups	white flour
1 cup	granulated sugar
1 tbsp	baking powder
½ tsp	nutmeg, grated
½ tsp	ground cinnamon
2½ oz	Crisco shortening
½ cup	milk

method

Preheat the oven to 350°F. Mix everything but the Crisco shortening and milk together in a large bowl. Using your hands, incorporate the shortening, kneading it into the dry ingredients until fully blended. Add the milk and stir with a wooden spoon until fully mixed. Drop the mixture by tablespoonful onto a parchment-lined baking sheet. Bake in the oven for 25-30 minutes or until lightly browned. Remove from the oven and cool for 10-15 minutes.

to serve:

Serve on a platter.

TRIO OF COOKIES
BY GILLES BALLAY

Cookies – always a favorite with adults and children alike. There is something for everyone with the choice of chocolate, peanut butter or oatmeal.

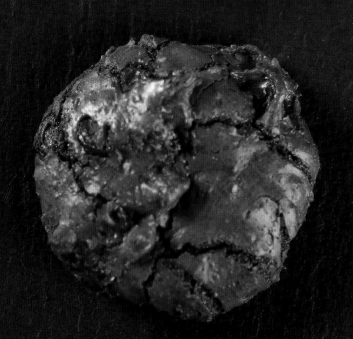

GILLES BALLAY

I was born in France and at the age of 16 I started in an apprenticeship with Jean Pierre Martin in Normandy. He taught me the basic principles of his profession: confidence, pride and passion in his work. In 1997 I moved to New York City and have worked there, in Las Vegas and Bora Bora. I met my wife while working at the Bellagio in Las Vegas and we now live in Thomaston, Connecticut.

As I'm now an Executive Pastry Chef there is one word that people use to describe my artisanal desserts and sweets — "Heavenly!". Mia, our two-year-old daughter, already has a refined palate for sweets and enjoys making cookies with me and messing up the whole kitchen!

Chef's tip:
Cookie dough can be made and frozen in advance.

TRIO OF COOKIES
BY GILLES BALLAY

makes approximately 50 cookies each

ingredients	method

cherry chocolate oatmeal cookies:

6 tsp	melted butter
¾ cup	brown sugar
1	egg
1 tsp	vanilla extract
⅓ cup	all purpose flour
⅓ cup	wheat flour
1½ cups	old fashioned oats
3 oz	semi-sweet chocolate
1 cup	dry cherries
½ tsp	salt
1 tsp	baking soda

peanut butter cookies:

8 oz	butter
8 oz	sugar
6 oz	brown sugar
2	eggs
few drops of vanilla extract	
8 oz	chunky peanut butter
13 oz	all purpose flour
pinch of salt	
½ oz	baking powder
4 oz	salted peanuts
caramelized nuts of choice as well as a few chunks of gianduja to place on top of the cookies (optional)	

chocolate dream cookies:

8 oz	unsweetened chocolate
1½ lb	sweet dark chocolate chips
6 oz	butter
11½ oz	all purpose flour
pinch of baking powder	
pinch of salt	
8	eggs
1½ lb	sugar
½ oz	instant espresso powder
1 oz	vanilla extract
1½ lb	chocolate chips

cherry chocolate oatmeal cookies:

Preheat the oven to 350°F low fan. Mix the butter with the sugar. Add the egg and vanilla extract then add the rest of the ingredients. Keep the dough in the refrigerator for at least 15 minutes. Place scoops of the dough on a parchment-lined cookie sheet and bake for approximately 12 minutes depending on size.

peanut butter cookies:

Preheat the oven to 325°F low fan. Using a mixer with a paddle attachment, cream the butter and sugars. Add the eggs and vanilla extract, then add the peanut butter. Add all the dry ingredients to make a dough. Scoop balls of desired size onto a cookie sheet lined with buttered parchment paper. Bake in the oven for approximately 12 minutes or until cooked. Place the caramelized nuts and gianduja decoratively on the cookies while they are still hot.

chocolate dream cookies:

Preheat the oven to 325°F low fan. Melt the unsweetened chocolate, sweet dark chocolate chips, and butter together. Mix the flour, baking powder and salt in a separate bowl. Using a mixer with a paddle attachment, beat the eggs, sugar, espresso powder, and vanilla extract until light. Add the chocolate/butter mixture at low speed. In increments add the flour mix to the egg/chocolate mixture until combined. Stir in the chocolate chips. Allow the mixture to fully cool then scoop desired-sized balls onto buttered parchment on a cookie sheet. Bake for approximately 12-15 minutes or until cooked.

to serve:

Allow the cookies to cool to room temperature or serve warm.

PORT CHERRIES

BY CHRISTOPHER KOSTOW

These cherries make a great, easy accompaniment to any full flavored cheese – they work equally well with a blue cheese as with a Cheddar.

CHRISTOPHER KOSTOW

I was raised in Chicago and attended Hamilton College in upstate New York. I've lived and worked abroad and enjoyed the experience very much from both a personal and professional standpoint. Although I'm not married and do not have any children yet, I do look forward to being a parent one day.

Cheese is just simply wonderful. It's something almost everyone enjoys and it's easy to prepare. In this presentation, the garniture we add gives it a little sophistication so it's a nice dish to prepare for guests when you're entertaining at home. My favorite ingredient? In terms of life, it's definitely humor. In terms of cooking I'd say great olive oil. My hobbies are reading; I'm always reading!

" cheese is just simply wonderful. It's something almost everyone enjoys and it's easy to prepare

PORT CHERRIES
BY CHRISTOPHER KOSTOW

serves 8

ingredients

1	bottle of ruby port (75 cl)
2	cinnamon sticks
3	star anise
10 oz	dried cherries

method

Place the port, cinnamon, and star anise in a pot and reduce the liquid by half. Pour hot over the dried cherries and let the liquid cool to room temperature before refrigerating. Store the cherries in the liquid.

to serve:

Serve with your favorite cheese.

A British classic that never goes out of fashion and is perfect for afternoon tea.

SCONES
BY BRIAN PORTEUS

serves 12

ingredients

8 oz	all purpose flour
4 oz	sugar
1 tbsp	baking powder
1 tsp	salt
4 oz	butter
1	egg
4 oz	milk

to serve:

berry preserve
clotted cream

method

In a large bowl combine the flour, sugar, baking powder and salt. Cut in the butter. Mix in the egg and milk until moistened. Turn the dough onto a lightly floured surface and knead briefly. Roll the dough to ½" thick, cut into the desired shape and bake at 390ºF for 15 minutes.

to serve:

Serve straight from the oven with berry preserve and clotted cream.

Because dining in our kitchen is a bit like dinner and a movie, we often serve this version of popcorn at the Chefs table. Don't knock yourself out looking for a truffle – that's what we're here for. Even without it this will be the best popcorn your guests have ever tasted.

TRUFFLED POPCORN

BY PATRICK O'CONNELL

serves 2

ingredients

to dress the popcorn:

¼ cup	raw popcorn
⅛ cup	melted butter
2 tbsp	good quality truffle oil
1 tbsp	fresh parsley, finely minced
½ cup	grated, aged parmesan cheese

salt & freshly ground black pepper, to taste

1	small, fresh, white or black truffle (optional)

method

Pop the raw popcorn in an air popper or in your favorite popcorn popper following the manufacturer's directions.

to serve:

Place the warm popped corn in a large mixing bowl. Toss the popcorn with the remaining ingredients. Keep the truffle to grate at the table.

INDEX OF RECIPES

Poussin

Roasted Milk-Fed Poussin with Guanciale, Caramelized Brussels Sprouts, Extra Virgin Olive Oil Potato Purée, Chicken Jus, *182*

Prunes

Duck Foie Gras with Prunes and Sugar Beet, *210*

Quail

Pan Roasted Carolina Quail with Sweet Potato and Leek Ragout, *198*

Rabbit

Rabbit Ragù with Pancetta and Olives, *214*

Radish

Dungeness Crab Cake, Radish and Wasabi Aioli, Asian Slaw, *30*

Ragout

Pan Roasted Carolina Quail with Sweet Potato and Leek Ragout, *198*

Poached Egg in a Ragout of Bacon and Chanterelle Mushrooms, *206*

Rice

Baked Stuffed Garlic Chicken with Jasmine Rice and Baby Spinach, *194*

Sushi Pizza, *92*

Ricotta

Ricotta Gnocchi with Truffled Crème Fraîche and Baby Tomatoes, *58*

Risotto

Risotto of Woodland Mushrooms and Roasted Celery Root, *20*

Sautéed Alberta Free Range Chicken Breast in its Own Jus with Morel Mushrooms, Pearl Onions, Smoked Bacon and Saffron Risotto, *202*

Saffron

New England Seafood Nage, Mussels, Littlenecks, Scallops, Cipollini Onions, Yukon Gold Potatoes, Fennel, Saffron, *80*

Sautéed Alberta Free Range Chicken Breast in its Own Jus with Morel Mushrooms, Pearl Onions, Smoked Bacon and Saffron Risotto, *202*

Salad

Beet Cured Salmon, Lemon and Celery Root Chutney, Caper and Jasmine Raisin Purée, Fennel Salad, *98*

BLT, *62*

Ham en Croute 'Papa Jo' and Fingerling Potato Salad, *178*

Potato Salad, *66*

'Raw & Cooked' Vegetable Salad, *50*

Salmon

Beet Cured Salmon, Lemon and Celery Root Chutney, Caper and Jasmine Raisin Purée, Fennel Salad, *98*

Scallops

New England Seafood Nage, Mussels, Littlenecks, Scallops, Cipollini Onions, Yukon Gold Potatoes, Fennel, Saffron, *80*

Pan Roasted Scallops, Sweet Corn Succotash, Fried Okra, *110*

Scones

Scones, *276*

Soup

Butternut Squash Bisque, *12*

Butternut Squash Soup, Roasted Pumpkin Seeds and Oil, *42*

Butternut Squash Velouté, Bacon, Crostinis and Chive Cream, *54*

Tortilla Soup, *26*

Spinach

Baked Stuffed Garlic Chicken with Jasmine Rice and Baby Spinach, *194*

Barron Point Oyster Gratin, Creamed Spinach, Parmesan Mousse, Pancetta Crisp, *16*

Sweet Corn

Pan Roasted Scallops, Sweet Corn Succotash, Fried Okra, *110*

Sweet Potato

Pan Roasted Carolina Quail with Sweet Potato and Leek Ragout, *198*

Tart

Litchi and Pink Grapefruit Temptation, *240*

Poached Pear and Hazelnut Frangipane Tartlet, *236*

Warm Granny Smith Apple Tart with Cheddar Cheese Ice Cream, *224*

Warm Mango Tart, *232*

Tomato

BLT, *62*

Grilled Beef Tenderloin, Marinated Grilled Vegetables with Smoky Tomato Vinaigrette, *144*

Tortilla

Tortilla Soup, *26*

Truffle

Poached Farm Eggs, Grits Cooked in Raw Sheep's Milk and Tennessee Black Truffle, *34*

Ricotta Gnocchi with Truffled Crème Fraîche and Baby Tomatoes, *58*

Truffled Popcorn, *278*

Tuna

Sushi Pizza, *92*

Veal

Braised Veal Cheek and Parsnip Purée with Bourbon Vanilla, *166*

Pappardelle Alla Bolognese, *116*

Vegetable

Grilled Beef Tenderloin, Marinated Grilled Vegetables with Smoky Tomato Vinaigrette, *144*

'Raw & Cooked' Vegetable Salad, *50*

Roasted Chateaubriand with Caramelized Root Vegetables, *140*

Roast Pork Tenderloin with Winter Vegetables, Thyme and Apple, *170*

Venison Ribs BBQ style with Winter Vegetables, *124*

Venison

Venison Ribs BBQ style with Winter Vegetables, *124*

Wasabi

Dungeness Crab Cake, Radish and Wasabi Aioli, Asian Slaw, *30*

Zeppoles

Zeppoles, *250*

INDEX OF PROPERTIES

For Reservations and Information, please call toll-free: 1-800-735-2478

■ RELAIS & CHATEAUX PROPERTIES IN NORTH AMERICA   ■ GRANDS CHEFS RELAIS & CHATEAUX

L'Auberge Carmel
Monte Verde Street at 7th Avenue
Carmel, California 93921
United States
Tel.:   + 1 831 624 8578
Fax: + 1 831 626 1018
E-mail: carmel@relais.com
Website: www.relais.com/carmel

Auberge du Soleil
180 Rutherford Hill Road
Rutherford, California 94573
United States
Tel.:   + 1 707 963 1211
Fax: + 1 707 963 8764
E-mail: soleil@relais.com
Website: www.relais.com/soleil

Auberge Saint-Antoine
8 rue Saint-Antoine
Québec City, Québec G1K 4C9
Canada
Tel.:   + 1 888 692 2211
Fax: + 1 418 692 1177
E-mail: antoine@relais.com
Website: www.relais.com/antoine

Biras Creek Resort
P.O. Box 54
North Sound, Virgin Gorda 1150
British Virgin Islands
Tel.:   + 1 284 494 3555
Fax: + 1 284 494 3557
E-mail: biras@relais.com
Website: www.relais.com/biras

Blackberry Farm
1471 West Millers Cove,
Walland, Tennessee 37886
United States
Tel.:   + 1 865 984 8166
Fax: + 1 865 681 7753
E-mail: blackberry@relais.com
Website: www.relais.com/blackberry

Blantyre
16 Blantyre Road, P.O. Box 995
Lenox, Massachusetts 01240
United States
Tel.:   + 1 413 637 3556
Fax: + 1 413 637 4282
E-mail: blantyre@relais.com
Website: www.relais.com/blantyre

Canoe Bay
P.O. Box 28
Chetek, Wisconsin 54728
United States
Tel.:   + 1 715 924 4594
Fax: + 1 715 924 2078
E-mail: canoebay@relais.com
Website: www.relais.com/canoebay

Castle Hill Inn & Resort
590 Ocean Drive
Newport, Rhode Island 02840
United States
Tel.:   + 1 401 849 3800
Fax: + 1 401 849 3838
E-mail: castlehill@relais.com
Website: www.relais.com/castlehill

The Charlotte Inn
27 South Summer Street, Box 1056
Edgartown, Massachusetts 02539
United States
Tel.:   + 1 508 627 4151
Fax: + 1 508 627 4652
E-mail: charlotte@relais.com
Website: www.relais.com/charlotte

Château du Sureau
48688 Victoria Lane
Oakhurst, Yosemite National Park,
California 93644
United States
Tel.:   + 1 559 683 6860
Fax: + 1 559 683 0800
E-mail: sureau@relais.com
Website: www.relais.com/sureau

Clifton
1296 Clifton Inn Drive
Charlottesville, Virginia 22911
United States
Tel.:   + 1 434 971 1800
Fax: + 1 434 971 7098
E-mail: clifton@relais.com
Website: www.relais.com/clifton

Cobblers Cove
Road View
St. Peter (Caribbean) BB 26025
Barbados
Tel.:   + 1 246 422 2291
Fax: + 1 246 422 1460
E-mail: cobblers@relais.com
Website: www.relais.com/cobblers

Daniel
60 East 65th Street
New York, New York 10065
United States
Tel.:   + 1 212 288 0033
Fax: + 1 212 396 9014
E-mail: danielnewyork@relais.com
Website: www.relais.com/danielnewyork

L'Eau à la Bouche
Hôtel-Spa-Restaurant
3003 Boulevard Sainte-Adèle
Sainte-Adèle, Québec J8B 2N6
Canada
Tel.:   + 1 450 229 2991
Fax: + 1 450 229 7573
E-mail: eaubouche@relais.com
Website: www.relais.com/eaubouche

Eden Rock – St. Barths
St. Jean
Saint-Barthélemy, French West Indies 97133
Tel.:   + 590 (0)5 90 29 79 99
Fax: + 590 (0)5 90 27 88 37
E-mail: edenrock@relais.com
Website: www.relais.com/edenrock

Eleven Madison Park
11 Madison Avenue
New York, New York 10010
United States
Tel.:   + 1 212 889 2535
Fax: + 1 212 889 0918
E-mail: eleven@relais.com
Website: www.relais.com/eleven

Esperanza Resort
Carretera Transpeninsular Km 7 Manzana
Punta Ballena, Cabo San Lucas (Baja
California) 23410
Mexico
Tel.:   + 52 62414 56400
Fax: + 52 62414 56499
E-mail: esperanza@relais.com
Website: www.relais.com/esperanza

Everest
440 South LaSalle Street
Chicago, Illinois 60605
United States
Tel.:   + 1 312 663 8920
Fax: + 1 312 663 8802
E-mail: everest@relais.com
Website: www.relais.com/everest

The Fearrington House Country Inn & Restaurant
2000 Fearrington Village
Pittsboro, North Carolina 27312
United States
Tel.:   + 1 919 542 2121
Fax: + 1 919 542 4202
E-mail: fearrington@relais.com
Website: www.relais.com/fearrington

The French Laundry
6640 Washington Street
Yountville, California 94599
United States
Tel.:   + 1 707 944 2380
Fax: + 1 707 944 1974
E-mail: laundry@relais.com
Website: www.relais.com/laundry

Gary Danko
800 North Point
San Francisco, California 94109
United States
Tel.:   + 1 415 749 2060
Fax: + 1 415 775 1805
E-mail: danko@relais.com
Website: www.relais.com/danko

Glendorn
1000 Glendorn Drive
Bradford, Pennsylvania 16701
United States
Tel.:   + 1 814 362 6511
Fax: + 1 814 368 9923
E-mail: glendorn@relais.com
Website: www.relais.com/glendorn

The Home Ranch
P.O. Box 822
Clark, Colorado 80428
United States
Tel.:   + 1 970 879 1780
Fax: + 1 970 879 1795
E-mail: homeranch@relais.com
Website: www.relais.com/homeranch

Horned Dorset Primavera
Route 429, km 30
Rincon, Puerto Rico 00677
Tel.:   + 1 787 823 40 30
Fax: + 1 787 823 55 80
E-mail: horneddorset@relais.com
Website: www.relais.com/horneddorset

Hotel Fauchère
401 Broad Street
Milford, Pennsylvania 18337
United States
Tel.:   + 1 570 409 1212
Fax: + 1 570 409 1251
E-mail: fauchere@relais.com
Website: www.relais.com/fauchere

Hôtel Le Toiny
Anse de Toiny
Saint-Barthélemy, French West Indies 97133
Tel.:   + 590 5 90 27 88 88
Fax: + 590 5 90 27 89 30
E-mail: toiny@relais.com
Website: www.relais.com/toiny

Hôtel St. Germain
2516 Maple Avenue
Dallas, Texas 75201
United States
Tel.:   + 1 214 871 2516
Fax: + 1 214 871 0740
E-mail: saint-germain@relais.com
Website: www.relais.com/saint-germain

Kingsbrae Arms
219 King Street
St Andrews, New Brunswick E5B 1Y1
Canada
Tel.:   + 1 506 529 1897
Fax: + 1 506 529 1197
E-mail: kingsbrae@relais.com
Website: www.relais.com/kingsbrae

The Inn at Dos Brisas
10000 Champion Drive
Washington, Texas 77880
United States
Tel.:   + 1 979 277 7750
Fax: + 1 979 277 7751
E-mail: dosbrisas@relais.com
Website: www.relais.com/dosbrisas

The Inn at Little Washington
Middle and Main Streets
P.O. Box 300, Washington, Virginia 22747
United States
Tel.:   + 1 540 675 3800
Fax: + 1 540 675 3100
E-mail: washington@relais.com
Website: www.relais.com/washington

The Inn of the Five Graces
150 East De Vargas Street
Santa Fe, New Mexico 87501
United States
Tel.:   + 1 505 992 0957
Fax: + 1 505 955 0549
E-mail: fivegraces@relais.com
Website: www.relais.com/fivegraces

Jean-Georges
One Central Park West
New York, New York 10023
United States
Tel.:   + 1 212 299 3900
Fax: + 1 212 299 3914
E-mail: jeangeorges@relais.com
Website: www.relais.com/jeangeorges

The Jefferson
1200 16th Street NW
Washington, District of Columbia 20036
United States
Tel.:   +1 202 448 2300
Fax: +1 202 448 2301
E-mail: jefferson@relais.com
Website: www.relais.com/jefferson

La Pinsonnière
124 Saint-Raphaël
La Malbaie, Québec G5A 1X9
Canada
Tel.:   + 1 418 665 4431
Fax: + 1 418 665 7156
E-mail: pinsonniere@relais.com
Website: www.relais.com/pinsonniere

Lake Placid Lodge
Whiteface Inn Road P.O. Box 550
Lake Placid, New York 12946
United States
Tel.:   + 1 518 523 2700
Fax: + 1 518 523 1124
E-mail: lakeplacid@relais.com
Website: www.relais.com/lakeplacid

Langdon Hall Country House Hotel & Spa
RR n°33
Cambridge, Ontario N3H 4R8
Canada
Tel.:   + 1 519 740 2100
Fax: + 1 519 740 8161
E-mail: langdon@relais.com
Website: www.relais.com/langdon

Las Mañanitas
Hotel Garden Restaurant & Spa
Ricardo Linares 107 Col. Centro
Cuernavaca (Morelos) 62000
Mexico
Tel.: + 52 777 362 00 00
Fax: + 52 777 318 36 72
E-mail: mananitas@relais.com
Website: www.relais.com/mananitas

Les Mars Hotel
27 North Street
Healdsburg, California 95448
United States
Tel.: +1 707 433 4211
Fax: +1 707 433 4611
E-mail: mars@relais.com
Website: www.relais.com/mars

Lumière
2551 West Broadway
Vancouver, British Columbia V6K 2E9
Canada
Tel.: + 1 604 739 8185
Fax: + 1 604 739 8139
E-mail: lumiere@relais.com
Website: www.relais.com/lumiere

Manoir Hovey
575 Hovey Road
North Hatley, Québec JOB 2CO
Canada
Tel.: + 1 819 842 2421
Fax: + 1 819 842 2248
E-mail: hovey@relais.com
Website: www.relais.com/hovey

The Mayflower Inn & Spa
118 Woodbury Road
Washington, Connecticut 06793
United States
Tel.: + 1 860 868 9466
Fax: + 1 860 868 1497
E-mail: mayflower@relais.com
Website: www.relais.com/mayflower

Meadowood Napa Valley
900 Meadowood Lane
St. Helena, California 94574
United States
Tel.: + 1 707 963 3646
Fax: + 1 707 963 3532
E-mail: meadowood@relais.com
Website: www.relais.com/meadowood

Montpelier Plantation
P.O. Box 474
Charlestown, Nevis, St Kitts & Nevis
Tel.: + 1 869 469 3462
Fax: + 1 869 469 2932
E-mail: montpelier@relais.com
Website: www.relais.com/montpelier

Patina
141 South Grand Avenue
Los Angeles, California 90012
United States
Tel.: + 1 213 972 3331
Fax: + 1 213 972 3531
E-mail: patina@relais.com
Website: www.relais.com/patina

Per Se
10 Columbus Circle 4th floor
New York, New York 10019
United States
Tel.: + 1 212 823 9335
Fax: + 1 212 823 9353
E-mail: perse@relais.com
Website: www.relais.com/perse

The Pitcher Inn
275 Main Street, P.O. Box 347
Warren, Vermont 05674
United States
Tel.: + 1 802 496 6350
Fax: + 1 802 496 6354
E-mail: pitcher@relais.com
Website: www.relais.com/pitcher

Planters Inn
112 North Market Street
Charleston, South Carolina 29401
United States
Tel.: + 1 843 722 2345
Fax: + 1 843 577 2125
E-mail: planters@relais.com
Website: www.relais.com/planters

The Point
P.O. Box 1327
Saranac Lake, New York 12983
United States
Tel.: + 1 518 891 5674
Fax: + 1 518 891 1152
E-mail: point@relais.com
Website: www.relais.com/point

Post Hotel & Spa
P.O. Box 69
Lake Louise, Alberta TOL 1EO
Canada
Tel.: + 1 403 522 3989
Fax: + 1 403 522 3966
E-mail: posthotel@relais.com
Website: www.relais.com/posthotel

Rancho Valencia
5921 Valencia Circle, P.O. Box 9126
Rancho Santa Fe, California 92067
United States
Tel.: + 1 858 756 1123
Fax: + 1 858 756 0165
E-mail: valencia@relais.com
Website: www.relais.com/valencia

Restaurant Initiale Inc.
54 rue Saint-Pierre
Québec City, Québec G1K 4A1
Canada
Tel.: + 1 418 694 1818
Fax: + 1 418 694 2387
E-mail: initiale@relais.com
Website: www.relais.com/initiale

Restaurant Toqué!
900 place Jean-Paul-Riopelle
Montréal, Québec H2Z 2B2
Canada
Tel.: + 1 514 499 2084
Fax: + 1 514 499 0292
E-mail: toque@relais.com
Website: www.relais.com/toque

Sonora Resort Canada
4580 Cowley Crescent
Richmond, British Columbia V7B 1B8
Canada
Tel.: + 1 604 233 0460
Fax: + 1 604 233 0465
E-mail: sonora@relais.com
Website: www.relais.com/sonora

Thomas Henkelmann – Homestead Inn
420 Field Point Road
Greenwich, Connecticut 06830
United States
Tel.: + 1 203 869 7500
Fax: + 1 203 869 7502
E-mail: homestead@relais.com
Website: www.relais.com/homestead

Triple Creek Ranch
5551 West Fork Road
Darby, Montana 59829
United States
Tel.:   + 1 406 821 4600
Fax: + 1 406 821 4666
E-mail: triplecreek@relais.com
Website: www.relais.com/triplecreek

Trout Point Lodge of Nova Scotia
189 Trout Point Road
East Kemptville, Nova Scotia B0W 1Y0
Canada
Tel.:   + 1 902 482 8360
Fax: + 1 800 980 0713
E-mail: troutpoint@relais.com
Website: www.relais.com/troutpoint

The Wauwinet
120 Wauwinet Road, P.O. Box 2580
Nantucket, Massachusetts 02584
United States
Tel.:   + 1 800 426 8718
Fax: + 1 508 228 6712
E-mail: wauwinet@relais.com
Website: www.relais.com/wauwinet

Wedgewood Hotel & Spa
845 Hornby Street
Vancouver, British Columbia V6Z 1V1
Canada
Tel.:   + 1 604 689 7777
Fax: + 1 604 608 5348
E-mail: wedgewood@relais.com
Website: www.relais.com/wedgewood

The White Barn Inn and Spa
37 Beach Avenue
Kennebunk Beach, Maine 04043
United States
Tel.:   + 1 207 967 2321
Fax: + 1 207 967 1100
E-mail: whitebarn@relais.com
Website: www.relais.com/whitebarn

Windham Hill Inn
311 Lawrence Drive
West Townshend, Vermont 05359
United States
Tel.:   + 1 802 874 4080
Fax: + 1 802 874 4702
E-mail: windham@relais.com
Website: www.relais.com/windham

Winvian
155 Alain White Road
Morris, Connecticut 06763
United States
Tel.:   + 1 860 567 9600
Fax: + 1 860 567 9660
E-mail: winvian@relais.com
Website: www.relais.com/winvian

Wickaninnish Inn
Osprey Lane at Chesterman Beach, P.O. Box 250,
Tofino, British Columbia V0R 2Z0
Canada
Tel.:   + 1 250 725 31 00
Fax: + 1 250 725 31 10
E-mail: wickaninnish@relais.com
Website: www.relais.com/wickaninnish

GLOSSARY

Al Dente

Meaning 'to the tooth', a slight resistance in the center after cooking.

Arzak Style

To line a ramekin with cling film and brush with oil, break an egg into the ramekin, close the cling film to create a bag with some air and poach in simmering water, turn regularly and remove from the bag; 'Arzak Style poached eggs'.

Baste

To cover with liquid before cooking; 'baste the roast chicken'.

Blanch

To transfer food to ice water to stop the cooking process; 'blanch the vegetables'.

Brunoise

To cut into a very small dice approximately 2mm x 2mm x 2mm.

Chinois

A conical sieve with an extremely fine mesh.

Confit

Food immersed in a substance for flavor and preservation.

Crostinis

Meaning 'little toasts', thin slices of bread, toasted, drizzled with olive oil, and served warm.

Deglaze

To use a liquid to remove cooked-on residue from a pan.

Dice

To cut into small cubes; 'dice the onions'.

Emulsify

To combine two liquids together which normally don't mix easily; 'Emulsify the water and oil'.

Ganache

A glaze, icing or filling.

Lardons

A small strip or cube of pork fat used in cooking to flavor foods.

Mandoline

Kitchen utensil used for slicing and cutting, especially into julienne (long and thin) strips.

Microplane

A perforated steel tool for grating.

Parisienne Scoop

A small tool used for scooping balls out of vegetables or fruit.

Pulse

To use an on-off mixing method; 'pulse the vegetables in a blender'.

Purée

To blend or strain cooked food until a thick consistency; 'blend until a purée'.

Ragout

A stew of meat and vegetables.

Ragù

A meat based sauce, often used with pasta.

Reduce

To simmer or boil a liquid until much of it evaporates, making it more concentrated; 'reduce the sauce'.

Render

To heat pieces of meat to produce fat that can be heated for cooking; 'render the bacon'.

Reserve

To keep to one side; 'reserve until serving'.

Sachet

Square of cheesecloth used to contain herbs and tied with butcher's twine.

Sauté

To fry briefly over high heat; 'sauté the onions'.

Sauteuse

A basic sauté pan with sloping sides and a single long handle.

Score

To cut shallow slits at regular intervals on the surface, 'score the meat'.

Sear

To brown quickly over very high heat, 'sear the meat'.

Shuck

To remove from the shell; 'shuck oysters'.

Silpat

A popular silicone mat used in baking to provide a non-stick surface without fat.

Skillet

A type of frying pan.

Sternum

A long, flat bone in the center of the chest to which the ribs are connected; 'cut along the sternum'.

Thermo Whip

A double walled stainless steel vacuum bottle with high insulation.

Velouté

A white sauce made with stock instead of milk.

CONVERSION CHART

Volume (Liquids)

1 teaspoon (tsp)	5 ml
1 dessertspoon	10 ml
1 tablespoon (tbsp) or ½ fl oz	15 ml
1 fl oz	30 ml
1½ fl oz	40 ml
2 fl oz	50 ml
2½ fl oz	60 ml
3 fl oz	75 ml
3½ fl oz	100 ml
4 fl oz	125 ml
5 fl oz or ¼ pint (pt)	150 ml
5½ fl oz	160 ml
6 fl oz	175 ml
7 fl oz	200 ml
8 fl oz	225 ml
(0.25 litre) 9 fl oz	250 ml
10 fl oz or ½ pint	300 ml
11 fl oz	325 ml
12 fl oz	350 ml
13 fl oz	370 ml
14 fl oz	400 ml
15 fl oz or ¾ pint	425 ml
16 fl oz	450 ml
(0.5 litre) 18 fl oz	500 ml
19 fl oz	550 ml
20 fl oz or 1 pint	600 ml
1¼ pints	700 ml
1½ pints	850 ml
1¾ pints	1 litre
2 pints	1.2 litres
2½ pints	1.5 litres
3 pints	1.8 litres
3½ pints	2 litres
1 qt	950 ml
2 qt	1 litre
3 qt	2 litres
4 qt	3 litres
5 qt	4 litres

Weight (Solids)

¼ oz	7 g
½ oz	10 g
¾ oz	20 g
1 oz	25 g
1½ oz	40 g
2 oz	50 g
2½ oz	60 g
3 oz	75 g
3½ oz (1 cup)	100 g
4 oz (¼ lb)	110 g
4½ oz	125 g
5½ oz	150 g
6 oz	175 g
7 oz (2 cups)	200 g
8 oz (½ lb)	225 g
9 oz	250 g
10 oz	275 g
10½ oz (3 cups)	300 g
11 oz	310 g
11½ oz	325 g
12 oz (¾ lb)	350 g
13 oz	375 g
14 oz (4 cups)	400 g
15 oz	425 g
1 lb	450 g
(½ kg) 18 oz	500 g
1¼ lb	600 g
1½ lb	700 g
1 lb 10 oz	750 g
2 lb	900 g
2¼ lb	1 kg
2½ lb	1.1 kg
2 lb 12 oz	1.2 kg
3 lb	1.3 kg
3 lb 5 oz	1.5 kg
3½ lb	1.6 kg
4 lb	1.8 kg
4 lb 8 oz	2 kg
5 lb	2.25 kg
5 lb 8 oz	2.5 kg
6 lb 8 oz	3 kg

Length

¼ inch (")	5 mm
½ inch	1 cm
¾ inch	2 cm
1 inch	2.5 cm
1¼ inches	3 cm
1½ inches	4 cm
2 inches	5 cm
3 inches	7.5 cm
4 inches	10 cm
6 inches	15 cm
7 inches	18 cm
8 inches	20 cm
10 inches	24 cm
11 inches	28 cm
12 inches	30 cm

Oven Temperatures

Farenheit	Celsius*	Gas	Description
225°F	110°C	Gas Mark ¼	Cool
250°F	120°C	Gas Mark ½	Cool
275°F	130°C	Gas Mark 1	Very low
300°F	150°C	Gas Mark 2	Very low
325°F	160°C	Gas Mark 3	Low
350°F	180°C	Gas Mark 4	Moderate
375°F	190°C	Gas Mark 5	Moderate, Hot
400°F	200°C	Gas Mark 6	Hot
425°F	220°C	Gas Mark 7	Hot
450°F	230°C	Gas Mark 8	Very hot
475°F	240°C	Gas Mark 9	Very hot

* For fan assisted ovens, reduce temperatures by 10°C

Temperature Conversion

F=9/5C+32
C=5/9 (F-32)

THIS GENERATION'S COOKWARE BREAKTHROUGH

*LTD*₂
WITH d5 technology™

All-Clad introduces patented d5 technology, delivering revolutionary performance and a lifetime of joyful culinary experiences. Now, for the first time, the exquisite LTD2 collection is dishwasher safe, in another breakthrough that will certainly make a splash.

A BOND WITH THE FUTURE
For more information, visit all-clad.com